THE LIBERATED CEO

THE
LIBERATED CEO

*The 9-Step Program
to Running a Better Business
So It Doesn't Run You*

SCOTT A. LEONARD, CFP®
FOUNDING PARTNER,
NAVIGOE, LLC

WILEY

Published by John Wiley & Sons, Inc., Hoboken, New Jersey.
Published simultaneously in Canada.

For general information on our other products and services or for technical support, please contact our Customer Care Department within the United States at (800) 762-2974, outside the United States at (317) 572-3993, or fax (317) 572-4002.

Wiley publishes in a variety of print and electronic formats and by print-on-demand. Some material included with standard print versions of this book may not be included in e-books or in print-on-demand. If this book refers to media such as a CD or DVD that is not included in the version you purchased, you may download this material at http://booksupport.wiley.com. For more information about Wiley products, visit www.wiley.com.

Library of Congress Cataloging-in-Publication Data:

Leonard, Scott, 1967–
  The liberated CEO : the 9-step program to running a better business so it doesn't run you/ Scott Leonard, CFP®, Founding Partner, Navigoe, LLC.
      pages   cm
  Includes bibliographical references and index.
  ISBN 978-1-118-65366-1 (cloth); ISBN 978-1-118-65355-5 (ePDF); ISBN 978-1-118-65332-6 (ePub)
      1. Strategic planning.   2. Business planning.   3. Management.   I. Title.
HD30.28.L454 2014
658.4'21—dc23

Printed in the United States of America.
10 9 8 7 6 5 4 3 2 1

CONTENTS

AUTHOR'S NOTES

This book references Mind Maps and material from www.thinkbuzan .com. Mind Map is a registered trademark of the Buzan Organisation Limited 1990, www.thinkbuzan.com.

In addressing the gender pronoun issue, I have chosen to use he/she and her/him interchangeably. I am deeply grateful to my world-class team at Navigoe for agreeing to be cited as examples in these pages.

PREFACE

When I first starting talking to literary agents about writing a book about my family's sailing trip, my idea was to write more of a work–life balance book that focused on living your dreams, and spending quality time with one's children while balancing the demands of a career. Soon into the process it became apparent that I had built my business in an incredible fashion. Sometimes intentionally, sometimes through luck, and many times through trial and error, I had created a system that allowed me to take my personal, individual relationships with my clients and migrate them to a personal, individual relationship with my company. This transition has been revolutionary for my company, and can be for any small business. So it is that we set out to take what I developed and learned over the years prior to our two-and-a-half year sailing trip into nine steps to help anyone transition their practice into a business, and liberate themselves from the day-to-day grind of the office. I hope you enjoy the lessons in this book and liberate yourself to go and live your dreams now.

ACKNOWLEDGMENTS

There are many, many people who have helped me bring this book to reality. Because so many have been so helpful, I am acknowledging people in their order of appearance in my life. My first thanks would have to go to my parents, for all the obvious reasons and more. In particular, I want to thank my mother, Kay D. Owens, who always supported my ideas and dreams, and never let my dyslexia and all the experts stop me from trying to live my dreams. She has played many other roles throughout my life, but specifically I am so grateful for her role as a business consultant in helping to set up and run my companies, even through today, where she functions as Navigoe's CFO. It was my father, Captain William Douglas Leonard, U.S. Navy, who first took me sailing on Lake Michigan. His passion for the water and sailing was contagious. As with many members of my family, he had the highest integrity and often spent long hours talking about right and wrong. He is sorely missed; I am sad he is no longer with us.

A book that came about due to a dream to sail could not have happened without the Ramsyer family. My best friend growing up, Kent, and his parents, Richard and Carol, were my gateway to sailing. I am sure the dream to sail around the world was discussed between Kent and me as we sailed around Alamitos Bay in Southern California. And

I am always indebted to Carol and Dick for letting Kent and me, plus Daniel Gregory, Michael Stea, and Jon Cruz, take their boat multiple times to Catalina. Those guys and the times we spent sailing are some of my fondest memories of high school.

It was also in high school that we purchased our Hobie Cat 16 and spent many a weekend sailing off the beach in Long Beach, California. My brother, William David Leonard, and those same high-school friends spent many a weekend seeing how many ways we could do a high-speed flip on the Cat. It is also those times that got me to love catamarans as our sailing boat of choice.

The support and love of my wife, Mandi Smith Leonard, is hard to fully acknowledge. When we first started dating, she lived in Northern California, which made the decision to move north and work for an investment management firm, RWB, much simpler. Once we were married, her support in helping me to launch and build Navigoe was critical. Her eagerness to take the family on a three-year sailing adventure allowed the dream to build for us all, and would not have happened without her support in so many ways. And her work on the trip, educating the boys, keeping us all well fed and healthy, and holding down the ship when I would travel back the States for work, goes above and beyond.

I want to thank Carl Reinhardt, Alan Werba, and John Bowen, the founders of Reinhart Werba & Bowen (RWB) for hiring me in Northern California so I could be closer to Mandi. From a business perspective, I am deeply grateful for the access they gave me to many of the financial services industry's first independent Registered Investment Advisor (RIA) firms, showing me that there is a way to work with individuals in the financial services industry with integrity and free of product sales. All three of the founders were excellent mentors to me in many ways.

When I first started my firm in Santa Monica, Robert Given, of Given and Associates, was kind enough to provide me with free rent and a nice office from which to work. More important, he was thoughtful and kind in helping me establish my messaging as a professional service firm. He was a true mentor in every sense of the word.

The growth of my firm has been greatly benefited by affiliation with a few professional organization. Dimensional Fund Advisors (DFA) and all their staff, affiliated academics, and fellow advisors have all been generous with their time and willingness to help in many ways. While it is unfair to single anyone out, certainly the founders of DFA, Rex Sinquefield and David Booth, as well as the brilliant academics Eugene Fama and Kenneth French, have had more influence over the investment strategies of my business than any other.

The independent broker–dealer firms of TD Ameritrade and Charles Schwab & Co. have both been instrumental in assisting firms like Navigoe to bring world-class offerings to our clients and to spend their resources to help us all build better, smarter businesses.

At Navigoe itself, I would like to acknowledge two very-long-term employees. First, I want to thank Melanie Dreike, who is one of the first persons I hired as I was building my company, and is still with the firm today. Additionally, thanks to Eric Toya, who was hired to be the primary advisor for our clients when I was on the sailing trip; he is now a partner in Navigoe.

Any mention of the company is not complete without acknowledging all the wonderful clients. Many of you have been an inspiration to live my life now, and not let the young years of my children's lives pass me by while I toiled away at the office. And for the willingness to let my experiment happen, and trust us to continue to provide the level of service you have expected while I was away from the office, I thank you all.

This trip never would have happened, or if it did, it would have been very different, without my three wonderful children, Griffin, Jacob, and Luke Leonard. It was challenging at times but, most of all, it was a time together that I hope we all cherish for the rest of our lives.

In preparation for the sailing trip, we had two very strong requirements that trumped all others. One was the medical training and supplies to feel we were not taking undue risks with our children's lives. To this end, we are so glad to have partnered up with MedAire (www.medaire.com), which provides medical training and supplies to both yachts and private aircraft. To complement the service, they have MedLink, a 24/7 hotline of physicians to help in any emergency or with any medical questions that arise.

The other requirement was communications. I needed to be always connected. We were fortunate to have the help of Frank August of Inmarsat and MVS USA (www.mvsusa.com), who helped us with the implementation of our satellite communications, and without their assistance our sailing trip would never have come to reality. As a result, we had worldwide coverage for phone calls and Internet access.

During the final stages of preparation for our trip, and during the trip itself, Beverly Visty of Dharmata Public Relations was very helpful in helping to promote our trip, which was a large contribution to eventually finding a publisher for our book. While on the trip, I was very fortunate to have the writing services of Zoe Alexander, who helped with the editing and wordsmith duties of my blog posts.

There were some early shakedown trips and needs to move the boat to stage for our adventure. Thanks are due to my brother David, brother-in-law Tyler Smith, and good friend Chris Smith for their trips to Florida and the Bahamas. A special thanks to Kevin McRoberts, who not only helped with shakedown trips, but often filled part requests back in the United States. Kevin was also forced to hear about my dream on all the sunset sails we took together on his boat *Menehuene* out of Redondo Beach in what seemed like a lifetime ago.

Lastly, this book would have never left my head and made it onto paper without the writing assistance of Herb Schaffner of Big Fish Media. From helping write my book proposal, to finding a publisher, to helping me synthesize my ideas into the written word, Herb has been an excellent partner.

I am very grateful to the generosity of a group of leaders who informed the development of this book, including Kathy Kolbe and the Kolbe Corp, Jennifer Goldman of Virtual COO, Anil Sekhri of Texas De Brazil, and Mark Tibergien and Rebecca Pomering for their book *Practice Made (More) Perfect.*

INTRODUCTION

SETTING FREE THE CEO (WHY A BUSINESS IS LIKE A BOWLINE KNOT)

As I write this introduction I've just finished a staff meeting under an 85-degree sun in the Caribbean, sitting on the deck of my 50-foot sailboat. My staff participated from multiple locations around the United States. The staff meeting was held via video conferencing; after chatting about where I was at the moment, and the need to move the computer's web camera around for a 360-degree view so everyone could see the beautiful surroundings, we got down to business.

This was not some emergency staff meeting that interrupted my family vacation. It was a scheduled check-in that I performed regularly during my two-and-a-half-year trip sailing around the globe with my wife and three children. We live together on the sailboat, working, exploring, and learning about the world. I'm the owner of a $3 million professional services firm and I am spending quality time with my family that few working parents are able to experience. Also, I am living one of my life's dreams, to sail around the globe, and I am getting to do it before I retire. All this, and I still run my business, Navigoe, LLC, that I created and enjoy immensely.

Scott at the Helm of *Three Little Birds*

Our firm is percolating nicely with our highest growth of assets under management, ever. I communicate with my management team as needed, from one to five times a week, and fly back to the office for quarterly meetings. I'm a liberated CEO, I'm a father and husband, and I'm a lifelong entrepreneur. Five years before our trip started, I began to prepare for this life change, and along the way I also made myself a better manager and leader than I ever expected to be.

Many entrepreneurs in professional services wouldn't want to leave their homes for two-and-a-half years to sail around the world. But we all have dreams and goals—from spending less time in the office, to taking a multiweek vacation, to retiring and transitioning ownership to a younger generation.

If you're like most entrepreneurs, you believe these goals are rewards that must be postponed until you've earned the right and the money to pay for them—after you've reached a particular financial target, sold your business, or retired. You likely believe your business will fail without your continuous involvement, even if you aren't the owner or CEO. You may be afraid that your colleagues and employees will make mistakes or the wrong decisions if given too much autonomy. You may wonder how you hire people with sufficient aptitude and integrity to work in your firm without you looking over their shoulders. You may have extracted yourself from micromanaging details on other folks' desks and started to focus on the urgent concerns of running a business—but wonder if you're heading in the right direction. You may be worried about the assets of your firm and whether your colleagues have created enough value to sell or merge. You may even be asking yourself, "What is next?" How will you turn your business into a stream of income for your retirement?

The *Liberated CEO* principles allow me to free myself from counter-productive details and distractions, to fulfill a goal of importance to my family, while meeting the highest management standards of my firm. You may not be interested in global travel or even taking a long lunch with your spouse. But, by using these principles, you'll transform how you manage and operate your professional services business so that you gain more control, freedom.

In this book, I'll detail strategies that remove the fears and anxieties of overmanaging and enable you to supervise your firm from just about anywhere and for any length of time. But the payoff is bigger than that. These processes will increase the efficiency of any professional service firm and most small businesses so you can work fewer hours, or earn more money than you may have thought possible. And here's a key for you and every leader in a professional services firm: Ultimately your business will be sold or merged and the value of that sale will determine a great deal about your personal wealth and the wealth of your employees and family members.

You can read this book today and make better decisions tomorrow; following these strategies consistently will help transform your business for the long run, so a successful transition of ownership is only the final leg of the profitable journey you've undertaken. The liberated CEO is always thinking like a seller, and you'll discover how that translates into tangible results right away. The liberated CEO is also remembering Steven Covey's famous second habit: Begin with an end in mind. As you go through the book, remember I welcome your questions and further conversation at our website, www.LiberatedCEO.com. I encourage you to take notes and save your questions to the end of the book, as we may answer many of them along the way.

My strategies enable leaders of professional services firms and other small businesses to become more efficient on multiple levels. The result is that you continue to provide customized, transparent services to your clients even as you grow. I call this smashing the service ceiling.

Whether you're a business owner, CEO, COO, or a budding entrepreneur, this book is going to teach you how to deliver world-class service customized to each individual client while empowering you to expand your customer base rapidly and with lower costs than you imagined. My system culminates with the principle known by the oxymoronic phrase, systematic customization. This breakthrough strategy leverages your valuable expertise as a business owner, principal, or manager, to institutionalize what clients love about you while enabling you to spend more time on new initiatives or personal goals.

I founded my financial services firm when I was just 28; it took many years of sacrifice, long hours, and frequent travel to make that happen. Somewhere in 2005, I began designing my company to allow me to spend three years sailing the world with my family. Back then, if retiring was an option, I probably would have done so. The astounding result today is that I have created a great business life for myself: one that I would do even if I didn't need the money. But the bigger discovery is this: What I have done can be replicated by anyone with entrepreneurial or executive responsibilities. The goal of this system and the book is not only to liberate the CEO but every committed professional seeking a career in professional services and many related businesses.

QUESTIONS AND ANSWERS?

As you go through the book, remember I welcome your questions and further conversation at our website, www.LiberatedCEO.com. I encourage you to take notes and save your questions to the end of the book, as we may answer many of them along the way.

SMASHING THE SERVICE CEILING

My liberated CEO solutions are like bowline knots. They are simple and quick to tie, extremely strong, and, when necessary, can be untied rapidly and easily. In other words, my processes are uncomplicated to implement yet powerful in their results. And most important, they can be abandoned very quickly if they are not working as expected. They are flexible.

This is best illustrated in terms of the quandary that confronts professional firms and many small businesses—the service ceiling. What do we mean by this? You started your business with a core of clients who wanted to work with you and sought your expertise. You put in long hours to provide great service to this stable of clients that loved and trusted you and referred more clients your way. Growing meant doing even more for some clients while acquiring new clients. Eventually, you began to see that ceiling looming above you: While each client should continue receiving the world-class service from you that they've always enjoyed, you're adding clients and services—leaving you less and less time.

The dilemma is universal for the growing service entrepreneur. Yes, you add professional staff, but if you grow too fast your expenses go up while your clients' satisfaction goes down because you're not available for them the way you used to be. The problem is exacerbated in that you have to spend more and more time managing the company and employees, and less time doing what you, and your clients, want—spending time together. Achieving the potential of your business seems to require giving less of your time to your best clients and more to marketing, management, and expansion. You may even have reached a stage where you would like to think about selling your business, but have no plans in place to ensure your clients will want to remain with the business after you leave.

The Liberated CEO shows you how to smash this service ceiling and continue to grow while maintaining high client satisfaction. In addition, *The Liberated CEO* does an excellent job of training the next generation of leaders and managers, who are then able to maintain and teach the strategies. Ultimately, our process frees you to work in your optimal zone of performance and reignite the passion that drove you to start your business and cultivate so many devoted clients.

The best-quality professional service firms are the small, boutique firms where the business owner is still working directly with clients. By liberating the CEO, small firms can grow and retain their boutique character. Our insights and strategies achieve similar results for small service businesses such as specialty retail stores.

The approach also speaks to the respect and trust that clients should expect to have in working with your firm. Look at the stock brokerage business, where personal relationships with clients have largely been abandoned in favor of a high-volume strategy based on selling branded-investment products without having in-depth knowledge of the customer and his or her concerns. Or consider global banking, where big brands have offices in every suburb, small town, and strip mall, but no longer emphasize local knowledge or relationships. Instead, they drive volume by selling investment products shaped by stringent, complex rules that can be gamed by some and leave other deserving citizens and businesses from getting financing. For too many big banks, the focus isn't on customer relationships but getting more "share of wallet." Legal and financial security are too important to be managed through point-and-click interfaces and one-size-fits-all solutions.

You'll see, for example, how my system can be used as a model to help put the words *personal* and *service* into the financial industry: personal financial services. Yet it is much bigger that just a single industry. My system can be used to improve the quality and service in almost any industry.

LIVING PROOF

I don't know about you, but a big reason I started my business, and one of the reasons most business owners start their own businesses, is to have the freedom and flexibility of not working for others. However, as is common with most successful business owners, I called the shots, making me critical to the day-to-day operations. As a result, I didn't have the freedom and flexibility I wanted in the first place.

You and I know that starting a business is a great deal of work. Many times entrepreneurs are taking substantial financial risks to get their businesses up and running. *The Liberated CEO* is about taking the successful business you have created, and turning it into a true company, one that can function in your absence and, if sold, would demand the highest multiples in your industry. Or, if you desire, it could continue to provide an income stream long into your retirement.

Most small to medium-size business go through similar business cycles, where they eventually decline as the owner looks to retire, spends less time in the business, or raids the coffers to create a retirement fund (see Figure I.1). *The Liberated CEO* is about continuing the growth through the maturity stage of the business, while allowing the owner to take a less active or different role in the day-to-day operations. This results in continued growth and never getting trapped in the maturity-to-decline stages of the cycle, leaving the entrepreneur free to pursue other activities.

Fortunately for my family, business, clients, and myself, I had this audacious goal of sailing around the world with my family. This goal forced me to do what was important, *even if it wasn't urgent*. It forced me to look forward and put specific goals and timelines down on paper. It forced me to create the model that I will discuss in these pages.

How do I know it works? I am living proof. I first started conversing with clients and divulging my plan when we were in the middle of the Great Recession. As you can imagine, it was not a good time to be telling clients that I was going to live on a sailboat for three years, especially when ours is a financial services firm. To say that it caused a great deal of anxiety from our clients would be an understatement.

I shared with them all the processes we put in place to allow me to take the trip and how it would not adversely affect them. I told them that my decision reflected a powerful fact about our company: We had engineered every process and system so we could serve our clients seamlessly even if the owner was out of the office for extended periods of time. As a result, it is a better, safer company for them.

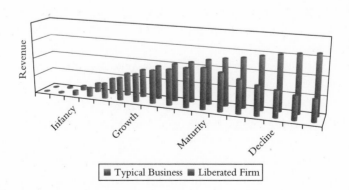

Figure I.1 The Typical Cycle of Small-to-Medium Sized Businesses Compared to the *Liberated CEO* Model

For those clients who threatened to fire us if I did take the trip, I responded by suggesting that before they go through the trouble of finding a new firm to work with, that they give it a chance and see if anything changes. If we were not able to maintain the same level of service, then we would help them find a new firm and refund the fees for the time I was on my trip. We were successful; not only have we kept every single client during this time, those (originally doubtful) clients have continued to refer new business to our firm.

At Navigoe, most new clients are referrals from current clients, so we use the stream of new referrals as a benchmark of our client satisfaction. During the trip, we expected referrals to cease, as I was the primary rainmaker for the firm. However, referrals have remained consistent. This is a great compliment to the staff of Navigoe and testament to the benefits of being a liberated CEO.

Our trip has been the ultimate test of the system. If the owner of a boutique financial services firm could literally sail away during one of the worst financial crises since the Great Depression, the system could hold up to just about any challenge.

In the fall of 2012 we were sailing through the French Polynesians in the island group called the Tuamoto Archipelago where we planned to drop anchor and explore for a few days. We had crossed over from extraordinarily deep water into a 25-mile lagoon, studded with coral reefs and miles of ribboned, white-sand beaches. The kids loved exploring the island over the next week (another sailing family had joined us)—climbing palm trees, battling each other with palm branches and coconuts, exploring the beach. While we knew the kids would have a blast, we were subdued because we knew that severe weather was moving into our area—big enough weather to interfere with satellite phone communications.

We had a scheduled conference call with one of our most important clients, an early supporter of mine I'd known for more than 10 years, for the next day. While we didn't know this beforehand, the client had booked the call to bring up a major concern, and he expected to have my full attention. By early morning, the storms had moved in faster than we expected, with high winds creating short chop, and dark clouds overhead. Before the call started, I had to move the boat across the lagoon to a leeward cove where we would be protected from the wind and wave chop. This required steering carefully through coral reef heads disguised by the waves and gray skies, avoiding their beautiful but steel-sharp formations that could tear a hole in our hull.

I dialed into the conference call, as I eased the boat across the lagoon. The air was warm with heavy humid wind. A little anxiety was building. Back in the California office, my number-two, Eric, was on the call as well. A moment or two after the call began I realized the longstanding client and friend was really upset about a mistake we'd made, and would require a significant response from us. He directed his questions to me, as well as his anger. Then, just a minute into the call, my satellite connection went down. I dialed back, and couldn't get through. By this time we had reached the cove, so I dropped anchor, and went below decks to our bedroom/office to focus on the emergency. I sweated away the thought that, just as many doubting friends had predicted, our trip was going to cost us major clients.

I punched in the number and the call still didn't go through. I was beginning to panic, and the commotion of our boys arguing in their room didn't help. I knocked on the bulkhead, "Guys, Daddy is on a business call, you have to keep it down!" I pulled out a notepad and kept dialing. I tried over and over. A few times I'd get a ring tone for a moment and then lose it. I pushed down the next fresh wave of panic even as I felt the embarrassment of being exposed as the liberated CEO who excelled at losing clients. After a half hour went by, I sighed, got a drink of water and wiped off the sweat. It was not an easy day in paradise.

After this, I fully expected to spend the next day or two salvaging the client's good faith and business and probably come up short. When I finally got through to Navigoe, the call had ended. It turned out Eric had handled the entire situation and the team wrapped up the meeting with a satisfied client. While I was melting down, the system I'd built for years delivered. Our training and processes fully equipped Eric, who had the poise and judgment to step up and work through the client issues without me. The relief was sweet and the self-analysis painful. After all, I had not trusted the system as I should have. However, this experience proved to be a stress test that told us it worked and could indeed be trusted.

Eric knew his number one responsibility was to keep the client happy. He heard out the client, addressed his needs and concerns, and assured him we're taking the right steps in the company so it won't

happen again. Eric knew he had the freedom to make his own decisions because he'd worked in our system for five years. Have you ever
had a crisis during a vacation or precious downtime that cost you a
client? I've lost clients in these kinds of circumstances in my earlier
years, and now it is not a concern I'll have again.

The system in this book is why the call ended well. The ultimate
proof of the steps you'll learn here is that they work in the real world.
In *The Liberated CEO*, you'll master the nine steps that empower you
to smash the service ceiling, and find a new work–life flexibility that
will give you control over your business and ownership of your life. To
preview the steps you'll be reading about:

1. **Chart your rhumb line—plot a three-dimensional
   vision.** In setting goals for your life and business, you need
   to take into account the curvature of reality, which includes
   family and personal concerns, external forces, and the difficulty of managing people. You also need to pre-test your plan
   for failure.
2. **Know your peak zone.** Our guidance for learning what you
   are best at, and only doing what you are best at—and managing
   your employees toward the same goal. Learn about the assessment tools that build effective teams.
3. **Smart sourcing. Hire the best—outsource the rest.** Our
   paradoxical approach to outsourcing for the professional services entrepreneur avoids common traps and liberates your
   firm to provide the highest levels of client service.
4. **Give your crew preflight checklists.** Learn how to embed
   critical processes and work flows into office software so each
   member of your team can focus on high-value work.
5. **Build a service brand.** How liberated businesses make customer awareness part of the fabric of every employee's job, so
   the client looks to the company as a service brand, not to the
   CEO. The results lead to sustained customer loyalty.
6. **Break the service ceiling with systematic customization.** How "vitals" worksheets, Mind Maps, and fast follow-
   ups bring together your technology and processes to deliver
   breakthrough results in efficiency and client satisfaction.

7. **Keep a loyal crew and the TLO secret.** Learn the power of managing employees to think like owners, and design your compensation to reinforce the strategy.
8. **Made to sell: Changing the watch.** Nailing your business's exit strategy is a major test for the liberated CEO; meeting the challenge ensures that the wealth you create is not dissipated by making the sale to the wrong buyer, or at the wrong time, or for the wrong reasons. We provide critical strategies for success.
9. **Become an expert in your field.** Why raising your profile as an expert, teacher, and/or thought leader is an amazingly productive benefit to living and leading as a liberated CEO.

THE NINE STEPS TO LIBERATION

1. Chart Your Rhumb Line—Plot a Three-Dimensional Vision
2. Know Your Peak Zone
3. Hire the Best, Outsource the Rest
4. Give Your Crew Preflight Checklists
5. Build a Service Brand
6. Break the Service Ceiling with Systematic Customization
7. Keep a Loyal Crew and the TLO Secret
8. Made to Sell: Changing the Watch
9. Become an Expert in Your Field

While each step represents a unique aspect of running your business, they all interact with one another. Each step is critical in helping ensure that the other steps are successful. I think of the steps as the fundamentals of running a business. Build, practice, and improve on one's fundamentals, and when it is game time it all comes together.

CHAPTER 1

CHART YOUR RHUMB LINE (PLOTTING A THREE-DIMENSIONAL VISION)

In this opening chapter, we guide you through the three stages of reaching your destination as a liberated CEO:

1. Establish a smart goal.
2. Pretest your plan for failure.
3. Build the milestones needed to attain your objective.

After all, without an endpoint, planning a route is kind of a waste of time. Or as the late management strategist and scholar C. K. Prahalad observed, "If you don't know where you are going, going faster doesn't help."

In establishing your vision, you and your business need a line of navigation to reach your future; sailing has taught me a useful metaphor for thinking about what this means. When plotting a navigational course on a map, it may seem that the shortest sailing route between two points is a straight line. But that's wrong. Even if that route is over open water, with no hazards to speak of, you don't sail on a flat line between A and B. You sail on what mariners call a rhumb line. This may be counterintuitive, but the shortest line between two points is in fact curved, since the two points are not on a plane, but a sphere—the surface of the earth.

THE TRUEST COURSE IS NOT A STRAIGHT LINE

In establishing your vision, you and your business need a line of navigation to reach your future; sailing has taught me a useful metaphor for thinking about what this means. When plotting a navigational course on a map, it may seem that the shortest sailing route between two points is a straight line. But that's wrong. Even if that route is over open water, with no hazards to speak of, you don't sail on a flat line between A and B. You sail on what mariners call a rhumb line. This may be counterintuitive, but the shortest line between two points is in fact curved, since the two points are not on a plane, but a sphere—the surface of the earth.

This concept is surprising to many of us who are accustomed to considering routes and distance in terms of maps, which are two-dimensional planes. The rhumb line is subject to calculations that are different for any point on the earth's globe: The actual curve you plot depends on the bend of the arc of your particular location.

In setting a line of navigation for your life and business, the metaphor of the rhumb line is quite fitting. When you choose your goal—the point B you want to reach from point A—it's unlikely you will reach that goal in a straight line—that is, by operating your business the same way, every day, with little variation—no matter how hard you work. You will need to take into account the curvature of reality, which includes all dimensions of life. Your life doesn't happen on paper. As with navigation, your experiences will not be governed by constant, unchanging circumstances, but by the curves and wrinkles of the unexpected.

I see the third dimension of business planning as the human element and this changes your calibrations on an ongoing basis. Does your thinking about your big goal incorporate the entrepreneurial fire and vision that spurred you into business, the attitudes of your clients, and the social and emotional needs of your loved ones?

To arrive at your vision, you must consider nonfinancial issues because ultimately you are not running and working in a business just for money. You have to ask questions about life in the long run as it involves your family, your community, and your financial aspirations.

PLAN IN THREE-D

Every executive or owner can talk about their big long-term goals at some level of specificity if given some time and a good cup of coffee. Do you want to make room for a family adventure or personal or spiritual quest? Do you want to reach a growth goal, then sell your business and retire to spend more time with family members? Do you want to start a related business while maintaining some form of leadership over the current firm?

THE ESSENTIAL QUESTIONS FOR A THREE-DIMENSIONAL BUSINESS PLAN

- What is the real deliverable of your business?
- What time investments will your family relationships and friendships require?
- What family transitions can you anticipate and plan for?
- What is the appropriate size of your contingency fund and how long do you need to build it?
- What is your end game?

Consider these questions in developing a three-dimensional business plan and goal:

- **What is the real deliverable of your business?** The late, great Peter Drucker famously observed that customers rarely buy what the company thinks they are selling to that customer. Why? Because "nobody pays for a 'product.' What is paid for is satisfaction." Or, as marketing guru Ted Levitt famously said to his Harvard Business School students a generation ago, "People don't want quarter-inch drills—they want quarter-inch holes."[1] All of us fall into the trap of thinking we are selling a service such as estate planning or real estate management or investment management, but in reality customers *hire* those products and services to achieve a goal. In my business, I realized after talking to many clients that our true deliverable is peace of mind. By answering this question, you'll gain focus on what is essential to your customer service. To gain insight into this question, pick out your five best clients and take them each out to lunch. Allow plenty of time. Ask them how your firm benefits them, and how your firm could improve in achieving that goal. Listen.

- **What time investments will your family relationships and friendships require?** Can you envision developments in this area such as seeing an aging parent one weekend a month, coaching a youth sport, starting a project with your children, or spending more time with your spouse on weekends?

- **What family transitions can you anticipate and plan for?** You've likely thought these through from a financial perspective. Have you considered what major transitions require in terms of your time? These events could be your spouse or close friend retiring or transitioning out from his or her career, an adult child's wedding or move, an aging parent's transition to an assisted-living facility, a philanthropic or community service commitment, a special-needs child progressing to high school or college, and so forth. Just as we plan and project for market changes in business, we should do so for our personal lives.

- **What is the appropriate size of your contingency fund and how long do you need to build it?** Whatever your liberation goal may be—from retirement, to introducing an innovative service, to spending more time outside of the firm—you want to carefully estimate what additional funds should be set aside as vision insurance to ensure that setbacks or unexpected new events don't hurt you or your firm financially.

- **What is your end game?** Very few of us can plan for our business, finance, and professional goals on the basis of business metrics only. You need to incorporate social, community, and family concerns, and your own purpose in becoming an entrepreneur when determining what your exit strategy is for your business.

By writing down answers for each of these questions you will be able to strengthen your goal, understand how it fits with your business, and plan for how long you need to reach it.

PRETEST YOUR PLAN FOR FAILURE

Experiencing failure is a necessary test for any ambitious venture. In the second stage of identifying your destination, you will test the highlights of your plan with your friends, trusted associates, and family. You're not setting out to run a survey or focus group. You're gathering feedback and ultimately support for a vision you have already decided is important (even if not everyone agrees with it). Don't include people whose opinion you won't take seriously. In my case, the ultimate plan was quite dramatic. In other circumstances, the goal may be less surprising (though just as important to you) and you'll improve your plan from the reactions and ideas your network feedback provides.

This stage has a few purposes. First, you learn from people you trust; second, you make a public commitment to your vision; and third, you give people in your network the advance education to prepare them so they are comfortable supporting you. Let's look at why these are important.

When you pretest your plan for failure, you collect all the reasons why you will not succeed. That way, you can evaluate them and determine which ones have merit, and which do not. Then, you focus on creating solutions to those possible roadblocks, before they appear. In this way, your advisors act as free business coaches who identify weak points in your thinking.

Our particular vision was a decade in the making. As we discussed it with friends and trusted advisors, we'd hear probing questions, such as, "Won't you have former employees stealing clients from you?" "How will you do crisis management when your systems don't work or you can't be reached?" "Won't your employees resent you for having this lifestyle while they do 'the real work?'" By answering these and many other challenges, we ended up implementing many of the steps that are now part of my *Liberated CEO* process.

The second purpose of this stage is that it ensures you will have witnesses to your plan, and that will help you stay the course. As we know from the success of Weight Watchers and Alcoholics Anonymous programs, peers are the most effective accountability partners. By pre-testing your plan through frank and trusting conversations, you're telling the people closest to you that you're going to make these changes. And, you're asking them to remind you of your goals and check in on your progress. Did you know Weight Watchers began with a New York City housewife, Jean Nidetch, who needed to lose weight and as she began losing motivation, recruited her friends to meet in their living rooms and lose weight together? Jean lost 75 pounds, made many new friends, and turned her experience into a company that ultimately went public in 1968, grew, was sold to other companies, and has prolonged the lives of millions of people.

As management consultant, relationship expert, and bestselling author Keith Ferrazzi wrote in his acclaimed book about peer accountability, *Who's Got Your Back*, "What's so extraordinary about all that? Jean just wanted to get skinny, but through an inner circle of friends offering expertise, wisdom, honesty, and support, she achieved far more than she ever imagined possible. Jean discovered what the great leaders and peak performers throughout history have always known: Exceptional achievement in work and life is a peer-to-peer collaborative process."[2] Your circle of pretesters act as what Ferrazzi calls "lifelines," an unofficial board of directors with whom you have candid, accountable discussions about your progress.

Whether you have accountability partners who check in via e-mail or in person, take advantage of the proven force of using peers to ensure we test, improve, and execute the changes we have planned. "What matters most to us is our relationship with fellow humans—the most commanding force for change," wrote journalist Tina Rosenberg in her acclaimed book, *Join the Club: How Peer Pressure Can Transform the World*, which documents the uniquely positive effects of the "social cure."

My plan had its roots about 10 years before our trip launched, with the implementation work starting 5 years before departure. (Part of our goal was to have our kids be as old as possible, but yet return home by high school.) With this much lead time, we had recurring accountability discussions—and many times our supporters doubted that we'd do our big trip at all.

Over the years, we realized a few key issues were paramount. The first issue was: Who will talk with and manage clients when the clients wanted to talk, in addition to my quarterly visits when I was back in the office? The answer? Hire someone. The second part of this solution was more challenging: Who would that be? How could we protect against that person taking our clients, failing to provide world-class service, or feeling resentment that they were doing all the work?

Our strategy to address these questions was executed in a series of milestones, the final stage in charting your rhumb line as a business leader and owner.

BUILDING MILESTONES

You can enact these strategies and tools in shorter (or even longer) time frames depending on the freedom, the goals, and the level of responsibility you wish to have. What's critical is segmenting your decisions along that time frame in milestones. Each milestone will help your business performance in real time as it is reached.

Each milestone prepares you to leverage more of your talent and time. If your big goal is to retire and transition your successful business to new family ownership, rushing the process can result in scaring clients who may pull some of their business away. If you are planning to take a three-year trip around the world, rushing the process could result in scaring your key employees who fear you'll never come back! Give each milestone the time it truly needs.

Writing down your milestone goals that need to be reached by certain times for you to reach your destination is essential to implementing the system in this book successfully. As we've said, the liberated CEO starts with the end in mind. As you know, my vision was to sail around the world. Now, that was not my ultimate endgame, but I knew this very important goal would require major changes to my business. I knew it would be critical to understand how these changes would be made over time, in the context of keeping our business strong.

One of the changes necessary was to have a relationship manager in the firm who could attend to clients in my absence. I decided I wanted at least two years with this person sitting in on every client meeting with me before I would start talking with my clients about my trip. Also, I wanted to give myself a buffer in case the first person I hired did not work out. So I decided that approximately five years before

I would leave on this trip, I would need to hire a relationship manager to work only with my clients. That milestone also involved revenue requirements for the firm, which translated into assets under management, which translated into the number of new clients I would need. I added extra time for particular milestones to allow for adjustments to unforeseen issues.

There were a number of these milestones. I put all of them, with the dates they needed to be attained, on a bulletin board in my office that I looked at every day. They weren't arbitrary business goals of increasing revenue by 10 percent a year, or adding a new client a week. They were the minimum requirements necessary for me to fulfill my dreams.

A great way to examine this concept it to look at some of the early milestones I created for Navigoe. The following is an extended example of the main goal and milestones I had on my bulletin board in my office:

Goal: Depart on sailing trip the summer of 2011. This requires:
- Relationship manager dedicated solely to my clients, with two years of experience working directly with them for at least two years before my departure. (This creates another milestone.)
- Have clients look to people in the company for their day-to-day questions, not me.
- Have clients view me as the big picture, strategic planner of the process, and the office staff as the implementation part.

Milestone: Hire an experienced relationship manager in first half of 2007. This requires:
- Additional cash flow to pay for the costs of such an employee, such as salary, profit sharing, and health care. (This was a big issue, as I was going to need to continue to receive my income to pay for my trip while in effect working much less in what was my traditional role in the firm.)
- In Navigoe, cash flow is a function of assets under our supervision; as a result, that had to increase.

Milestone: Hire additional support staff. Time as needed, but staff to be employed by 2011.
- Requires cash flow for additional employee, which should be in correlation with the need for the additional work.

Milestone: Add another $50,000 of pure profit before hiring relationship manager in Spring 2007.

Milestone: In 2006, have all clients look to the office first for answers to their on-demand questions.

- At the time, I called this making myself intentionally irrelevant to the day-to-day operations of the firm. This milestone caused me to develop the concept that became systematic customization, covered in Chapter 6 in this book.

Milestone: Add another $50,000 of pure profit to the firm by end of 2005.

- This milestone would prepare us to hire the relationship manager. At the time, I estimated this to be around $10,000,000 of additional assets under supervision, but that turned out to be an underestimation. This is a good example of a milestone that had to be adjusted along the way.

The revenue milestones have even more milestones or accomplishments tied to them. While revenue milestones are common with most businesses, mine were tied to a strong desire to take the trip with the family. I had put in place the minimum I needed to accomplish to keep my plan on course. I believe whole heartedly that having the revenue goals tied to a concrete and personally meaningful goal encouraged me to do the unpleasant and difficult tasks necessary to make it a reality.

As you can imagine, there are a great number of steps that need to be accomplished along the way to reach a milestone. However, I like planning through a big-picture lens, so identifying the milestones and why they needed to be completed was as much detail as I could commit to paper. I was still learning as I went along. Many of the nine steps in this book were created as a result of reaching the milestones.

When plotting a course on a two-dimensional map, you plot multiple turns along the way—in effect, the rhumb line. The same is true about building out the milestones. When looking at the end goal, the milestones are all the little turns that you are required to reach along the way. In sailing terms, these are called waypoints. While the waypoints are plotted on the chart, seldom do you actually cross over the very spot in the ocean marked by the waypoint. This is a result of all the different issues affecting your progress toward that single way-point. This fact of navigation causes a constant need to recalculate the rhumb line along the way. In other words, the waypoints are constantly changing to adapt to the circumstances affecting your progress.

The need to constantly update one's heading along the rhumb line is automated by the software in modern chart plotters and Global Positioning Systems (GPS). As we discuss in later chapters, the use of technology is critical in the automation of your business to help you reach your milestones and manage the course of your business.

Take this analogy to setting up milestones. They are the accomplishments to be reached when striving toward a goal. But the accomplishments are seldom realized as designed, which in effect causes the need to constantly change the milestones along the way to reaching the end goal. The whole process becomes cyclical. As milestones change and are adapted, new items need to be run by friends and the plan needs to continue to be tested.

Your business is going to grow and change during the process, and if you choose the best roles and responsibilities for yourself and your team, you may reach your milestones faster than you thought, particularly if you are working in your peak zone.

CHART YOUR RHUMB LINE: KEYS TO THE CHAPTER

In setting a line of navigation for your life and business, the nautical metaphor of the rhumb line is quite fitting. When you choose your goal, it's unlikely you will reach it in a straight line—that is, by operating your business the same way, every day, with little variation, no matter how hard you work. You need to take into account the curvature of reality as you plan, in three stages:

1. Establish a smart goal by reflecting and incorporating key family and personal needs and transitions, establishing a contingency fund, and considering your exit strategy.
2. Pretest your plan for failure with trusted associates, family, and friends.
3. Develop and write down milestone goals that need to be reached by certain times in order for you to reach your destination.

NOTES

1. Scott Anthony, "3 Ways To Predict What Consumers Want Before They Know It," *Fast Company*, www.fastcodesign.com/1669070/3-ways-to-predict-what-consumers-want-before-they-know-it. Excerpt from *The Little Black Book of Innovation: How It Works, How to Do It* (Boston: Harvard Business Review Press, 2012).
2. Keith Ferrazzi, *Who's Got Your Back?* (New York: Crown Random House, 2009).

CHAPTER 2

KNOW YOUR PEAK ZONE

As we discussed in the previous chapter, I ran into the occasional doubter about the financial sense of our worldwide sailing trip. We also heard from well-meaning people about the riskiness of it all. Putting my family out on the open seas with no access to hospitals, schools—not to mention In-N-Out Burger or Starbucks!—is courting disaster, in the views of some. (To reassure you, we take medical preparedness seriously, have advanced medical training, and subscribe to MedLink and MedAire, a concierge medical service, to which we have constant access through digital and satellite phone connections using Inmarsat's Fleet Broadband—to learn more about our experiences, see Appendix 1.) There's little doubt that Mandi and I share an adventure gene and thrive on new experiences. We're extremely tame and careful compared to some extreme sport enthusiasts, such as mountaineers (though I've summited Mount Rainer and a few other smaller peaks).

Extreme mountaineering provides a good analogy to the challenges of becoming a successful entrepreneur. If you're familiar with the reporting about the business of climbing Mount Everest, you might know what I mean. Hundreds of climbers converge on Everest with Sherpas (local Nepalese expert guides) and tons of equipment every brief climbing season. On Everest the area above the last staging area at South Col is known as the death zone, since the altitude, dangerous conditions, and low oxygen levels won't allow human beings to survive for more than 48 hours there, even with oxygen support. More than 150 unrecovered climbers' bodies are scattered over the death zone and the various ascent routes to the peak, because many of them froze or fell to their demise in ways that makes their recovery impossible.[1] One area along the northeast route to the summit has earned the nickname of Rainbow Valley, simply because of "the multicolored down coats of the numerous remains littering the hillside. In the severe conditions of lethal altitudes, corpses can remain for decades, some appearing frozen in time with climbing gear intact."[2]

Nonetheless the challenge of ascending the world's tallest and deadliest peaks attracts ambitious climbers willing to risk death to achieve their goal. Macabre details aside, I like the analogy to successful entrepreneurs. Entrepreneurs and founders of service businesses also possess the ability to tolerate substantial risk and have the inner drive to scale difficult and remote pathways to reach the highest levels of achievement.

The entrepreneur wants to operate in his or her peak zone, moving toward the summit, doing the work he or she is best at, and staying out of the dead zone where they are not contributing value. Climbers seeking to reach the peak of Everest can only wait in the death zone for a short period of time before making the ascent to the peak. The longer they wait in the death zone, they weaker they become to make the final climb. The goal for the entrepreneur should be the same. If a task is not in your peak zone, then it is in your dead zone, and you need to stop doing it as soon as possible.

As with mountaineers and Sherpas, peak entrepreneurs must learn how to work with the experts on their own team. Just as a climber cannot reach the peak without a highly trained team to map the ascent, cart supplies, and set up rope lines, the entrepreneur must hire the best people whose strengths complement his or hers, so they can focus on reaching the summit.

Every climber in the Himalayas knows how valuable it is to have great Sherpas who literally know the ropes about the best routes to the summit. The Sherpas have scaled Everest many times; they set the ropes and ladders every mountaineer uses to reach the peak. This allows the climber to save her energy and attention for the most dangerous and demanding part of the ascent through and above the dead zone. This is how a liberated CEO's team should work—with each member of the team performing the tasks that sets up the leader to do the high altitude work she does best.

It is well known that many businesses fail because entrepreneurs find it difficult to transition from the skills that gave them success in their careers, into the roles they must perform in managing, growing, and leading a business. This inability to make a transition out of unproductive activities will trap the professional services entrepreneur in a career death zone, stalling progress because the wrong people are doing the wrong tasks—including you.

You must discover, know, and operate within your peak zone. This zone is defined by the work you truly like and where your strengths lie. And if you're not working in your peak zone, you're in your death zone.

The peak zone model is truly indispensable to the *Liberated CEO* model—assuring that leaders, managers, and administrative staff are aligned with jobs that fit their skills, strengths, and work styles. The metaphor of the peak zone works in so many situations—and it can be your secret weapon as a manager.

THE PEAK-ZONE MANAGER

Let's face it; most entrepreneurs are not great at managing other people. You became an entrepreneur because you did not like being managed. You are a self-starter, hard worker, and fully motivated to see your business succeed. You are passionate about your service or product. It is a passion that allows you to be successful where others have failed. However, few employees are as passionate about the business as the owner.

Even fewer employees have the skills, self-motivation, and drive of the business founder or principal. It should be no surprise that most entrepreneurs find it difficult to see the need to motivate employees and provide the constant positive reinforcements many employees require. If the management of people is not in your peak zone, either find workers who do not need managing, or hire a manager.

However, peak-zone management is about more than the ability to delegate by hiring someone to do what you don't like doing. The owner and founder must spend as much time in his or her peak zone as possible as the business grows. The people you hire must also work in their own peak zones, and you need to understand what those are. That's the unbeatable model for creating a productive, peak-performing team.

The peak-zone manager must learn the answers to these questions:

1. What is your peak zone?
2. How do you hire great employees that blend into a strong whole by complementing and counterbalancing your assets?
3. How do you know you can trust your people to perform at their best?

FINDING YOUR PEAK ZONE

Determining your own peak zone, and staying out of your dead zone, should be considered one of the great accomplishments of starting and building one's own business. One of the most rewarding aspects of being an entrepreneur is getting to do what you want, and only having to do what you want. It is truly one of the best measures of success, far more important than the size of your wallet. What is ironic to me is that people tend to be most successful doing the activities that they truly enjoy. So in effect, finding the financial and personal success you want becomes less about work, and more about operating in your peak zone.

I am not suggesting that as the business owner you are able to delegate all the tasks that you do not enjoy. However, the more time you spend in your peak zone and out of the dead zone, the happier and more successful you will become. I find there are two secrets to finding and maintaining this state of high performance: being honest with yourself and determining the best use of your skills.

In high school, students go through a process to determine their individual skills in addition to their likes and dislikes. This process is what got me started thinking about finance and/or sales as a career. What I find interesting is that until I had started my own firm and was getting some coaching assistance, I had never gone back and done any self-assessment of my strengths and weaknesses. It is a systemic failure of Western business philosophies that we do not do more assessing of our strengths and abilities in the workforce. We'll go into more detail about this shortly.

The process of defining your peak zone can be one of the most freeing experiences for the entrepreneur. We all have had, or still have, items on our to-do list that never seem to get completed. We look at these items and beat ourselves up for not getting them completed. Most likely, many of the tasks you're struggling to complete are ones in your dead zone. By understanding that you are not well suited to these tasks, you free yourself to hire someone else to perform these tasks for you. Letting go of the dead zone items on the to-do list frees up your time to do what you want and enjoy doing. This freedom will allow for more happiness than any other traditional form of measuring success.

As I am writing this book, I am finishing up the final months of my sailing adventure with my family. The trip has been an amazing experience. In some ways it has far exceeded expectations, and in others it has been a little disappointing. My experiences will fuel more of my writing in the years ahead. One of the subpar aspects of the trip was how much I was being forced to operate in my dead zone.

Whenever I am back in the States working, I always get the question, "So, how is the trip going?" Internally, I am thinking that it is just okay. I would not want to say that out loud, since it is hard to explain why, so I say, "Great!"

It was in putting this chapter together that I realized why my internal readout of the trip is a little flat. As the owner of a successful company, I have been working in my peak zone for many years. I forgot about all the dead-zone work I had to do in order to reach the level I have in my company. My sailing trip is like a new company, where I am responsible for doing a great number of different tasks, many of which are in my dead zone. Understanding this has allowed me to realize why my attitude was not great, and to focus less on the drudgery of the dead zone and more on the joy of the peak zone. That's how it is for those of you with younger firms—there's more drudgery, but the goal of the peak keeps you going and gives you the glimpses of joy you'll have when you reach it.

So now when I am asked how it is going, I truly believe it has been great, with the asterisk that it takes a lot of work doing a lot of activities I really do not enjoy, but it is all worth it.

As you build your firm, you know every aspect of operations requires your involvement—from marketing to customer management to finance. You also know that your customers came to you for your talents in your peak zone—whether it is accounting, investment management, legal representation, communications expertise, or estate planning. This is what your firm is all about, and if you insist on retaining day-to-day control of functions such as billing or marketing when your firm is adding clients, you will lose touch with the winning attributes of the business that fueled its growth. By letting go, you paradoxically stay in touch with everything your company truly is about.

For example, one of the great aspects of our firm is our investment philosophy. What makes it so successful is also what makes it complicated and difficult to understand; it is based on decades of academic research and statistics but lacks a short, simple explanation. By letting go as I've done on our sailboat where I'm geographically and psychologically removed from the day-to-day distractions, I can thrive at finding new ways to explain our strategy in simple language. I am free to spend the hours necessary to counter the sound-bite media hype of the investing world with short and compelling presentations, one of my better skills. This behind-the-scenes consideration of client concerns helps to ensure I am on top of my game when I return to the office to meet with clients.

Changing your mindset is an important development; hiring the right people is the next giant step.

HIRING A BLENDED TEAM

As we discuss in the next chapter, you should only hire full-time staff for roles that touch your customers, whether this is office management, client management, marketing—what have you. Each person you hire should be expert in their area; second, they should have work and leadership styles that complement yours. Delegating is really about effectively allocating roles to the people best equipped to do them. This also relates to hiring and managing decisions.

We view cognitive and behavioral assessments as a crucial tool, if you understand and know how to use them. Many firms—particularly midsize and large firms—incorporate assessments into the interviewing and hiring process to counter the biases many of us have when we hire. Our view of this is a little different and definitely grounded in common sense. You need to know your own strengths, tendencies, skills, and decision styles before you hire people to join your team on an outsourcing or insourcing basis. And you need to hire people who will do the jobs you won't and shouldn't do.

Our firm has benefited by working with the team at Kolbe Corp., founded by scientist Kathy Kolbe and led by CEO David Kolbe and President Amy Bruske. They have researched and developed the predictive and insightful assessments based on the Kolbe Concept, called the Kolbe Indexes. These tests have a lot in common with ideas in the so-called strengths movement that is very popular in human resources and corporate training and development circles. Many firms use Gallup's StrengthsFinder 2.0, for example, or other tools such as the Career Anchors Self-Assessment, developed by Edgar Schein at MIT's Sloan School of Management.

Assessments tend to measure personality and emotions, such as Myers-Briggs, or cognitive strengths, such as an IQ or aptitude test. The Kolbe assessment tools measure our instincts and natural ways of taking action, the whole collection of talents and drives that from how we operate. Kolbe calls this our conative nature, defined as "the aspect of mental processes or behavior directed toward action or change and including impulse, desire, volition, and striving." If you're familiar with the phrase modus operandi, or M.O., this captures what Kolbe means by the conative.

As noted on the Kolbe website, she "was the first to identify four universal human instincts used in creative problem solving. These instincts are not measurable. However, the observable acts derived from them can be identified and quantified by the Kolbe A Index. These instinct-driven behaviors are represented in the Four Action Modes®:

1. Fact Finder: the instinctive way we gather and share information.
2. Follow Thru: the instinctive way we arrange and design.
3. Quick Start: the instinctive way we deal with risk and uncertainty.
4. Implementor: the instinctive way we handle space and tangibles.[3]

Conative testing tends to have strong predictive value in show-ing where you'll be successful and productive as opposed to where you'll struggle to meet expectations because work tasks and processes require you to go against the grain of your strengths and inclinations. I am not a social scientist, but certainly there's more than one type of assessment that can help you build a team with complementary strengths. We suggest you find a great tool and use it consistently because it'll force you to be honest with yourself and understand the real reasons why you're hiring or outsourcing talent. Explore the Kolbe assessments in more detail in our sidebar Q&A with Kathy Kolbe on page 35.

The experience of using the Kolbe A™ (as well as asking other questions about qualifications and temperament) confirms what I've learned from being in firms earlier in my career where I was asked and pushed to perform in areas that weren't a good fit for my drives and skills. If I was going to make the most of my abilities, I needed to understand myself, and I didn't want to hire or work with people who were just like me. In order to operate in the peak zone, any profes-sional's job needs to be consistent with their normal M.O.

"You have to know yourself before you know how to manage other people," Kolbe told me in an interview. "You also need to understand in the same way your own team and the clients, the people you're pro-viding products and services for. Most people fail because they don't know themselves very well."

Kolbe tests help support and reinforce our philosophy of build-ing a blended team. For example, I am effective and energetic about research, innovation, big ideas, taking the initiative; Melanie, my executive assistant, is extremely strong on follow through and execu-tion. Her drives and talents in working tasks step-by-step and ensur-ing that each day's priorities are addressed is so important that her job description includes directing me to stay on track with client needs and my schedule, and when necessary, to call me out on an important deadline.

I am a strong Quick-Start type, as described by the Kolbe A Index, possessing the drive to come up with all kinds of new and "better" ways to work and make changes within our firm. I have learned that it is best for me to sit with the Implementers in the company and talk through the idea and process. The process is powerful on many different levels. First, it forces me to think through all the implications a change would have on the staff of the firm; this has helped me many times to understand that it is not as simple for the staff to implement as it is for me to come up with the idea. More important, if my idea passes muster with the office, then there is buy-in from the whole team, and especially the Implementers, who will end up bringing the new idea into action. Not only does this process substantially help to improve teamwork in the firm, but it also allows all employees to feel empowered to criticize the owner's "idea of the week."

This kind of synergy works with other teams in our firm, as well, and with many firms who use Kolbe and similar instruments. Many experts like to talk about collaboration and how important it is. I wholeheartedly agree—if it's effective collaboration. And for that collaboration to be effective, you need to work in your peak zone while each of your colleagues does the same. "I preach collaboration," Kolbe told me. "There are 12 conative strengths, and no one has more than 4. We were created to be interdependent; we can never succeed as much individually as we will collaboratively. No one should be so arrogant as to think they can do it all—because they can't." Wise counsel for those seeking the path of the liberated CEO!

If you're an office comprising one or two principals in early stages of making a key hire, remember that you need to know what you want new team members to do so you can work in your peak zone. Keep these suggestions in mind:

- Keep a time log of how you and anyone else associated with the firm spends their professional time. You can find software apps that make this fairly routine.
- Create a list of duties and tasks that need to get done in your organization. Analyze how professional time is being used and which of these functions are taking up a significant amount of time.
- Group together the tasks and duties that fit together for a single position. All activities that constitute a position should fall well within a proper modus operandi or for our firm, a proper Kolbe Index. Finally, make notes about the strengths and skills that suit that particular position.

- As you prepare to interview candidates, you may want to work with a consultant such as Kolbe or Gallup or read their books and materials to improve the interview process.

By doing what you are best at and encouraging others to do the same, you'll find managing people far more satisfying and rewarding.

TRUSTING THE ROPES

Peak-zone managing works because you're going to be most efficient doing what you like to do. And doing what you like to do means providing world-class service to your customers. To return to our earlier metaphor, you need to concentrate on the climb to your firm's goal, not whether the ropes are in the right place or tied with the right knots. You need to trust the ropes. If you're looking over your shoulder down the mountain, you'll lose your focus. To stay in the peak zone, you must allow your team members to have true ownership over their roles.

In terms of human behavior and performance, micromanaging throws off the balance of your team; if you have a leader who is a high-scoring Quick Starter interfering with an office manager who is a high-scoring Implementor, you may end up with an okay result but waste time, good will, and energy getting there. As a manager, you need to set goals, review progress, and communicate about developments in the business. Even in senior management roles such as hiring, recruitment, finance, branding, and thought leadership, you must never assume your way is the only way.

You'll read in later chapters how to use methods such as checklists, mind maps, customer-relationship management software, and outsourcing to provide an open-source structure for monitoring your team's progress against business goals and priorities. As noted by Kathy Kolbe, "When people act according to instinct, their energy is almost inexhaustible—like water running downhill. But when people are forced to act against their instinct, their energy is rapidly depleted—like water being pumped uphill."[4]

KATHY KOLBE ON THE CONATIVE MIND AND THE ENTREPRENEUR

Source: Photo by Heather Hill; permission of Kolbe Corporation.

Q: How does the Kolbe A Index compare and contrast with other instruments such as Myers-Briggs and StrengthsFinder?

Kolbe: Assessments fall into three types, based on how they test different parts of the brain. Many tests such as Myers-Briggs test affect—the emotional realm. Myers-Briggs is based on a Jungian scale of different affects such as introvert to extrovert. The test is asking questions that seek to know whether you have a preference for doing one thing as opposed to another. A second category of assessments are cognitive, and test learned behavior and acquired skills. The findings of cognitive tests such as the IQ are variable for individuals; that is, they are

(continued)

subject to change depending on factors such as age, gender, and cultural background. Cognitive tests tend to be unfair to people who haven't had equal educational opportunities. Neither cognitive nor affective tests are reliable in predicting how people will behave at work.

The Kolbe Indexes were developed after I realized each of us operates with a predictive pattern of actions that reflects how we react, interact, and take action; this is our modus operandi, or M.O. Our modus operandi (M.O.) reflects a unique pattern of striving instincts, an internal unchanging drive that creates energy. We can't measure instinct but we can observe and measure the actions that result from those instincts. Conative testing is far more powerful in predicting how we'll act and react.

Q: What are common mistakes made by business owners and entrepreneurs when it comes to managing and hiring?
Kolbe: Many people who lose their jobs in the corporate world and decide to start a business are making a mistake because they don't possess the characteristics our research identifies are absolutely essential to being a successful entrepreneur. In my research we can predict entrepreneurial success quite reliably. You need a Quick-Start score of 7 or more—and that needs to be higher than your Fact-Finder score. People who don't have this M.O. can still work in their own business, but should explore different models such as partnerships.

Most important, once you start a business or become an executive, you need to know yourself; you need to really take a look in the mirror, before you know how to manage other people. You also need to understand your clients, the people you're providing products and services for.

Business owners make a common mistake of hiring people they like and are like them, which means they'll all share the same strengths while having too many missing methods. This is the kiss of death. We recommend using our RightFit program which will ensure you don't only hire people you like, but the people you need to be successful. You'll also get conative diversity, which is the most important kind of diversity and brings with it the generational, gender, and racial diversity so critical to businesses today.

Q: How can Kolbe Indexes help business owners and leaders make the right hires for their team?
Kolbe: Our Leadership Analytics Reports are all about decision making—what role should you play in your company, and should you

change that role? If you're leading a company, you need to have the right M.O., the right combinations of attributes. And you need to know what kind of qualities your team needs so your staff members are actually working together, not operating independently while receiving a paycheck from the same bank account. Our assessments will give you an in-depth understanding of when to bring in the right people, of what work you should be in, and what work you should get out of.

There are 12 Kolbe Strengths. Everyone has four, one in each Action Mode. We were created to be interdependent; we will never succeed as much individually as we will collaboratively. It doesn't matter how good you are at one thing; success in one realm doesn't translate to everything that you need to do in a business. No one should be so arrogant as to think they can do it all—because they can't.

There's so much to gain by having the courage to look at yourself and others around you and accept and use the truth, rather than hide from it. If I could only know one thing about myself, about my personality, I would want to know my innate abilities, and that's what the Kolbe Index does for you.

KNOW YOUR PEAK ZONE KEYS TO THE CHAPTER

Extreme mountaineering provides a good analogy to the challenges of becoming a successful entrepreneur. Founders of service businesses possess the ability to tolerate substantial risk and have the inner drive to scale difficult and remote pathways to reach the highest levels of achievement. The liberated entrepreneur wants to operate in his or her peak zone, moving toward the summit, doing the work he or she is best at, and staying out of the dead zone where she is not contributing value. These strategies keep your team operating within each person's peak zone:

- Use assessments to deepen self-awareness and better understand strengths, abilities, and inclinations.
- Hire a blended team, by incorporating tests and predictive assessments from firms such as Gallup or the Kolbe Corporation.

(continued)

> By establishing a shared set of measures for people's strengths and methods of operation you help ensure that you allocate roles and responsibilities to people best equipped to do them.
>
> • When your team is in place, trust your team members to do their work and don't micromanage. As with any great mountaineer, trust the ropes other experts have put in place for your ascent.

NOTES

1. "Abandoned on Everest," *A Sea of Lead, A Sky of Slate* (blog), April 5, 2010, http://godheadv.blogspot.com/2010/04/abandoned-on-everest.html.
2. Ibid.
3. Kathy Kolbe, Kolbe Corp., www.kolbe.com/why-kolbe/kolbe-wisdom/four-action-modes/, accessed April 1, 2013.
4. Kathy Kolbe, Kolbe Corp., www.kolbe.com/theKolbeConcept/the-kolbe-concept.cfm, accessed April 1, 2013.

The trademarks listed are the trademarks of Kathy Kolbe and Kolbe Corp. All rights reserved. Used herein with permission.

CHAPTER 3

SMART SOURCING: HIRE THE BEST—OUTSOURCE THE REST

In our economic era, you have the advantage of choosing from an abundance of highly reliable experts and contractors available for virtual services. The reality is we live in an economy driven by on-demand labor because of the enormous cost advantages delivered by this evolution.

Global spending on business-process outsourcing in the financial and accounting industries will exceed $25 billion in 2013, and rise at an annual rate of 8 percent through 2017, according to a recent analysis by HfS Research and accounting giant KPMG.[1] The outsourcing revolution is about far more than vendors outside our country providing IT, technical, or administrative services. For small businesses and professional services firms, outsourcing is now a just-in-time, flexible-workforce strategy for bringing experts into your business when and where you need them.

Among the most common moves: outsourcing administrative functions such as marketing, bookkeeping, and IT services. The basic benefits of the approach are clear: Limit your full-time employees to those who are truly essential to operate your business and keep full-time employees with the costs and headaches off your books. But there's something missing from most of the small and professional services business literature: detailed advice on how to make these decisions to drive the vision and goals of your business.

Some have adopted the strategies of bestselling author Tim Ferris, whose system preaches outsourcing life's annoyances and distractions to give you more personal freedom. I'd be careful about taking that too far. I'm not sure I agree with giving a virtual assistant working for modest fees the responsibility of managing my most important relationships and responsibilities.

Others get excited about the allure and benefits of hiring a marketing or technology guru and then misspend the dollars or mismanage the consultant. Once burned, some owners become resigned to going back to the traditional path of doing extra work on nights or weekends or stealing time from client services.

Others outsource their answering service and stop there. The receptionist is often the customers' first point of contact with a financial planning firm, doctors' office, or accounting service. Customers form first impressions from the professionalism and expertise of those who interact with them. The receptionist is often the first person to greet and contact clients and prospects—so you should be careful about outsourcing this function to a call center or automated system.

The liberated CEO's approach to outsourcing avoids these traps. You and your core team members need to operate in their peak zones so your clients will continue to receive the unique mix of expert advice and reliable services that is your firm's reason to be. Outsourcing's value lies not only in its cost effectiveness, but in the flexibility it affords you in ensuring that you use every possible moment of your time and that of your team members' time working for the success of your clients. "The people you hire and bring in-house should think like owners who care about everything in the firm," notes Jennifer Goldman, a CFP®, founder of My Virtual COO and an innovator in business operations who has advised us on automating our business systems. "Every staffer is someone who can be fully ingrained into your business."

This analyzes the four factors you must consider in hiring outside experts and blending them with your team. These are:

1. Managing costs.
2. Focusing on customer touch points.
3. Competing on knowledge.
4. Managing your outsourced team for accountable results.

First, let's start with most obvious condition for these strategies.

THE HIDDEN COSTS OF FULL-TIME STAFF

It is obvious that hiring full-time staff is a major cost consideration for every business. While having great people on your full-time team will ultimately determine how fast and far you journey toward your goals, having the wrong people can turn the lights out on your plans faster than you imagine. The first step to making sound decisions in hiring is to understand all the important costs embedded in hiring those W-2ers.

When you decide to hire, you may invest in a talent agency or recruiter, which involves a small percentage of their first-year salary. You will have the costs of having staff write a job description and of the time involved in staging interviews and screening candidates. The expenses of onboarding and training an employee can be considerable. You may need to purchase training or management seminars. I estimate the cost of training and onboarding a professional employee to approximate $3,500. In addition, full-time staffers add to overhead costs such as computer terminals, desks, chairs, square footage, and utilities.[2]

Naturally, you have the costs of payroll taxes, health care, vacation, and contributions to their retirement accounts. You have the investments of your time managing new people, particularly if your hire is not the good fit you thought. If they can't perform their duties as you had planned, other staff may have to do their work and become less satisfied. Their dissatisfaction can be exposed to your clients.

Every time you have to let go of an employee who didn't work out or didn't like working at your firm, that employee will talk about your firm in the community. If that discussion is negative, your firm's reputation can suffer. For professional service firms, your community is a major source of clients and client referrals. Of course, there are times in the life cycle of any business that parting ways with an employee is necessary and the benefits far outweigh these concerns. However, this is an outlay to consider in the evaluation process. I make these points to confirm that a fulltime hire is first, last, and always a strategic proposition that speaks to the fundamental health of your firm.

While in-house, full-time employees come with the issues just raised, they are also the employees over whose actions you have the most control, and most important, they will have many interactions with your clients. Consider every aspect of how a prospective employee will react to and manage your clients.

INSOURCE CUSTOMER RELATIONSHIPS

Outsourcing is not about your company becoming less personal and responsive; rather, paradoxically, it is a strategy that strengthens your customer relationships. Outsourcing allows you to hire the skills and capabilities you need to serve your customers, while having constant, highly responsive control over costs. Outsourcing should improve client loyalty and satisfaction, not erode it.

If you outsource client management and service activities, clients and vendors will notice. Their satisfaction and trust will erode over time. If you outsource conversations with your clients to India, it is likely your clients will outsource their business to your competition down the street. Creating a blend of insourced and outsourced talent is about how you maximize the efficiency of each person in your firm to recruit and retain clients. Looked at another way, your outsourcing suppliers are a kind of farm team allowing you to call up the role player you need for your lineup to play for a few games or in a specialized task.

Here's the axiom: You don't outsource tasks because it's easy and it's cheaper in the short run. You outsource what you shouldn't be doing because those noncore tasks interfere with advising and serving your customers.

Anyone who's great at customer service and engagement is going to be extroverted and thrive on connecting and building relationships. Whether we're talking about receptionists, customer account managers, marketers, or principals of the firm, the people who love working with customers aren't likely to be effective working in an office all day on financials, bookkeeping, or PowerPoint decks. (That's another strategic reason you have to segment tasks so people are working in their peak zones.) It may be difficult to identify these personality types in outsourced situations.

Some executives (and I've done this) seek to avoid more labor costs by trying to spread some of the extra dead zone work among a number of staff employees in hopes they'll complete it when they have some spare time. But inevitably their performance with clients and their core tasks begins to suffer, because they process this kind of work slower, and find it demoralizing. As we know from our partnership with Kathy Kolbe, when people work away from their conative strengths, they process slower and procrastinate more.

To tap the potential of outsourcing in meeting your firm's goals of growth and profitability, develop models to get a strategic picture of how your choices will change your business' financial picture. If you invest in hiring outside experts, where will you save other staff costs? If you free up additional staff time to focus on customer services, recruitment, and sales, what growth will you project over the next year? Can you foresee your team devoting additional hours to bringing in new business? As we discuss in Chapter 8, providing ownership in your firm to your permanent employees is key because as you sculpt each job to fit your team members' peak zones, you need your team to take advantage of the opportunity to serve customers and bring in business.

Always view outsourcing as a strategic lever for reaching business goals, not as a solution in itself. That's why it's also important to remember the financial advantages of having the right people inside your firm working as committed staffers. These include predictability (your contracted experts can unexpectedly shift more of their time to another client, cut back on needed hours, or take a full-time job), protection of your competitive secrets and intellectual property, reduced training and onboarding costs, and having a team approach to customer service and management.

These advantages diminish with high turnover. Research by the think tank Center for American Progress examined 30 case studies on the costs of employee turnover and found that it costs businesses about one-fifth of a worker's salary to replace that worker—and an even higher percentage for more skilled employees.[3] An in-depth analysis of best practices in analyzing and managing employee turnover published by the Society for Human Resource Management and authored by David G. Allen of Fogelman College said that turnover is particularly troublesome for small businesses: "Turnover matters for three reasons: (1) it is costly; (2) it affects a business' performance; (3) it may become increasingly difficult to manage."[4]

WATCH YOUR TURNOVER

Smart outsourcing helps reduce turnover, a significant cost for smaller companies, as noted in *Retaining Talent: A Guide to Analyzing and Managing Employee Turnover*, by David G. Allen and published by SHRM.[5]

Turnover is tougher on small organizations: The loss of key employees can have a particularly damaging impact on small organizations:

- Departing workers are more likely to be the only ones possessing a particular skill set or knowledge set.
- A small company's culture suffers a more serious blow when an essential person leaves.
- There is a smaller internal pool of workers to cover the lost employee's work and provide a replacement.
- The organization may have fewer resources available to cover replacement costs.

To avoid high levels of turnover, you need to reward your core, full-time staffers appropriately, and that includes benefits and flexibility. By using smart outsourcing strategies, you retain the workflows that suit your team's strengths and firm's strategies.

In liberated businesses, full-time employees are highly valued and often part owners of the firm. Exercise care in outsourcing the human resources, workplace, and compensation issues that are critically important to them. Just as you build loyalty with clients by understanding and addressing their concerns, do the same with the care and feeding of your hard working team. If possible, define a role for a full-time employee who will act as a human resources sounding board and office manager, even on a part-time basis. This will help ensure your staff members are treated well and taken seriously.

COMPETING ON KNOWLEDGE

Smart sourcing is a way to stay abreast of best practices and industry knowledge. By aligning with experts you can fill technical or strategic gaps in your operational knowledge. We've found this strategy to be a huge difference-maker. When you partner with consultants who are expert in a particular issue, they typically work with your competitors, and can share what they've learned elsewhere. For example, we were struggling to understand how to develop certain kinds of reports and metrics from the software platform we use to manage client financial portfolios. We reached out and hired the firm that developed the software to consult with us occasionally. By doing so, we not only improved our client reporting and market responsiveness, but held sessions with the proprietary experts who taught us deeper levels of flexibility and analysis within the software we hadn't understood previously.

You'll discover that outsourcing to firms specializing in your own industry's proprietary software or business processes is particularly productive. These outside experts become more than just doers and implementers; they become best-practice experts by leveraging their collective experiences from serving their clients. As with all customer-service firms, the quality of your advice improves as you gather more experience and knowledge. When you consider outsourcing even tactical or short-term work, such as upgrading a software package or performing a marketing campaign, select from vendors who have many clients in the same industry; this makes it possible for your team to learn about best practices among competitors, and adapt and improve the service your firm provides. However, your hires should offer more than the robotic completion of tasks; you want someone willing to consult on the best way to perform the tasks.

When we were searching for the perfect boat for our family's trip, my wife and I flew to meet with a boat maker in China to explore having a semicustom boat made for us. The advantage of China is the low-cost labor, which is a major part of the cost of a cruising sailboat. During the weeklong visit in China, and conversations with others who have built their own boats, we realized that having the boat built in China would not be good for our needs. One of the aspects of the Chinese culture that helps them to be such great manufacturers is the unquestioning work ethic of the people. These are hard-working people willing (or pressured to) work long hours on all the routine and repetitive work involved in manufacturing at lower costs than found in many Western nations. The trade-off of this culture is that employees tend not to question the tasks they are assigned.

When building a semicustom boat, there is a good amount of mundane handwork necessary. However, such work needs to be completed with experience and questioning as to its function and appropriateness. In other words, all tasks need to be questioned, which is not part of the manufacturing culture of China. Their culture also tends to hinder the process of learning from past mistakes or leveraging the experiences of multiple semicustom projects.

Even if the task you are outsourcing is a mundane, repetitive task, you want to work with a firm that is learning and improving upon the process. The outsourcing partner should demonstrate the drive to question your process and recommend improvements. The result is that they not only help in completing a task, but create and share the best practices around that task.

If you're in a law firm, rather than simply bottom-source the completion of routine legal documents such as wills or articles of incorporation, consider hiring the document experts to consult with your team on improving document preparation and execution as clients experience it. If you're operating a physician's practice, talk to your peers about the consultants they've used to improve administrative and office practices, for example.

MANAGING THE EXPERTS FOR ACCOUNTABLE RESULTS

Smart sourcing doesn't end with hiring the consultants and experts. Many owners of professional services firms make a rookie mistake of assuming their hired experts require minimal oversight. Liberated CEOs need a checklist to vet their outsourcing decisions. You need to interview your candidates, check references, and set up weekly discussions to review work progress and priorities.

In an interview, Jennifer Goldman of My Virtual COO said, "Many leaders assume that outsourced workers know what are your top priorities on the to-do list. What we recommend is don't microman-age your outsourced team; instead, macromanage them. Hold regular phone meetings and integrate communications into your CRM so their tasks, your priorities, and communications are as transparent as those for onsite staff. You want to always keep your experts on the same page with you. We strongly recommend entering all your com-munications, tasks, and to-do lists involving outsourced workers in the same system that your onsite staff is using."

Goldman also says that failure to budget realistically is a common problem, "You have to be honest about your budget for an outsourced worker, who is usually paid by the hour, and project your costs accu-rately. Too many owners are not aware of the true hours it takes to complete certain tasks, or place a temporary limit on the hours of work allowed to control initial costs.

"They also forget to allot their own time to discuss how tasks will be done and if it matches their expectations, and forget to schedule regular check-ins with the outsourced worker. This leaves them with the feeling that they're throwing money in the wind and feeling surprised with the invoice when the surprise could have been avoided."

A customer relationship management (CRM) software system is no longer an option for professional services firms; it is a must. A CRM provides an office-wide shared platform for making and tracking all customer communications, activities, needs, and next steps. Because the CRM tracks and stores all the data you enter, it provides invaluable information at a glance. As Jennifer Goldman notes, "in addition to the ability to increase efficiencies and grow a profitable business, a CRM can serve as a critical compliance component, allowing advisors and their staffs to log all activities in a compliant way."[6]

Since we're discussing CRM, let me say I agree with many lead-ers in our field that Microsoft Outlook cannot stand in for the CRM systems available now. Outlook has functions of CRM, and many times is part of a CRM system; however, it is not a CRM system in itself. If your answer to "What CRM system do you use?" is "None," "Outlook," or "What is CRM?" then you need to find a firm that specializes in your industry to help you implement a robust CRM system. The best way to find such a firm is to look to your professional association and peers for references.

HOW IS CRM DIFFERENT FROM MICROSOFT OUTLOOK?

Way better! You can collect far more data with a CRM system than with Outlook, and do more with that data. You can tailor your data collection and classification to your industry. If you've stuck with e-mail list builders, a true CRM system will be a wonderful relief. With financial advisors, for example, the relationships of a contact to other contacts is key—children, grandchildren, other family members. In our CRM system we are able to segregate data in categories that include:

- Client segregation (A, B, and C clients)
- Goals
- Client associations (school, church, charity)
- Key extended family members
- Assets
- Net worth
- SS#
- Tax rates

All this data can then be searched and queried for clients in many different ways, and you can ask the CRM to perform any number of tasks. As an example, say we want to send an e-mail to all our A clients who have IRA accounts with a value in excess of $100,000 and are over the age of 70. Our CRM system would create a list of the clients and the account number of the IRA account(s) that meet the criteria. Then if we wanted, we could have the system do a mail merge and e-mail those clients a semicustom e-mail. Try doing that with Microsoft Outlook!

Assuming your data is correct, this whole process can be completed in minutes. If the purpose of the e-mail was to remind the client that they needed to do this year's Required Minimum Distribution from their IRA, a follow-up action item could also be automatically set for each client, and then in a week, month, whatever, if the items were not completed, you could run another report. Maybe this was done for all clients, but the B clients get a follow-up e-mail while the A clients get a follow up phone call. The bottom line is that if you can think it, you can probably do it with a CRM.

CRM is one aspect of managing the outsourcer relationship, including training these vendors in special concerns regarding client confidentiality, financial integrity, and communications guidelines. Keep these practices in mind to ensure your "insourced" and smart-sourced teams are equally compliant and working to the same standards; as described and with thanks to Amy Buttell's excellent 2012 article in *NAPFA Advisor Magazine*, "Nine Ways to Embed Compliance When Outsourcing to Virtual Staff":[7]

- Have consultants trained to use your customer relationship management software to ensure they are using up to date, compliant, and correct client agreements and other common documents.
- All outsourced staff should work under a contract and nondisclosure agreement, no exceptions.
- If you're outsourcing tech support, web security, or software management that involves financial or legal transactions, ensure your vendors have tech security and privacy protections that meet state and federal regulatory requirements.
- Develop workflows and protocols for smart-sourced staff as well as in-house staff. "Most advisory practices have developed repeatable workflows for some client-related tasks," notes Buttell, ". . . these firms often don't put the same level of attention into tasks they manage with outsourcers. Investing the time to quantify a process and enter it into the CRM or other technology will save time down the road. It will cut the costs of compliance, too . . . "[8]
- Use secure communication platforms with outsourcers. Avoid sending confidential documents by e-mail; use cloud-storage services, such as DropBox, that are controlled on your server.

As we will discuss in Chapter 6, the operating model for liberated firms is systematic customization. Outsourcing is a cornerstone of that strategy. Outsource as much of your operating systems as you can, so the firm can provide the customization. The customized offerings and expert advice you offer are the reasons clients come and want to work with your firm. The next chapter introduces the importance of automated workflows and checklists for your in-house staffers.

SMART SOURCING KEYS TO THE CHAPTER

Outsourcing is widely misunderstood and misused but is a key competitive advantage for professional services firms if deployed to better serve your long-term business goals. The paradox of smart, cost-effective outsourcing is that it does not lead to your company becoming less personal and responsive; rather it strengthens your customer relationships. Liberated CEOs outsource based on these four factors:

1. Managing costs—too often outsourcing costs more than is expected.
2. Focusing on customer touch points—you want clients to hear and know the professionals who answer the phone, manage their business, and answer their questions.
3. Competing on knowledge—outsource to leading experts in their specialty so you can stay ahead of the innovation curve.
4. Managing your outsourced team for accountable results.

NOTES

1. *Finance and Accounting BPO Market Landscape*, HfS, KPMG Shared Services and Outsourcing Advisory Practice, 2013, www.kpmginstitutes.com /shared-services-outsourcing-institute/insights/2013/pdf/hfs-fao-study-2013-summary-methods-only.pdf.
2. David J. Drucker and Joel P. Bruckenstein, *Technology Tools for Today's High-Margin Practice* (Hoboken, NJ: John Wiley & Sons, 2013).
3. Glynn Boushey, "There Are Significant Business Costs to Replacing Employees," Center for American Progress, Washington, DC, November 16, 2012, www.americanprogress.org/issues/labor/report/2012/11/16/44464/ there-are-significant-business-costs-to-replacing-employees/.
4. David G. Allen, *Retaining Talent: A Guide to Analyzing and Managing Employee Turnover* (Alexandria, VA: Society for Human Resources Management, 2008).
5. Ibid.
6. Jennifer Goldman, "CRM No Longer an Option for Advisory Firm Growth," *The Trust Advisor*, January 28, 2013, http://thetrustadvisor.com/ wealth-tech-news/crm-no-longer-an-option-for-advisory-firm-growth.
7. Amy Buttell, "Nine Ways to Embed Compliance When Outsourcing to Virtual Staff," *NAPFA Advisor*, July 2012, 26.
8. Ibid.

CHAPTER 4

GIVE YOUR CREW PREFLIGHT CHECKLISTS

As you make decisions about the great people who join your team, you need to give them the right tools to perform at their peak. The employees you hire to do what you can't or don't want to do are not copies of you. Liberated CEOs hire qualified professionals to perform essential high-level duties. They nurture employees, respect their roles, and give them autonomy to perform those roles.

This is also achieved by supporting staff with smart processes that managers and staff co-create and document in checklists. This step derives from my view that each employee in your business should have guidelines for the day-to-day and week-to-week processes of their job. I see this as akin to the preflight checklists used by pilots in air or sea.

I'm not suggesting that businesses create more procedure manuals that employees return to the shelf after they have earned their wings. This is something different. When a pilot prepares for a trip, she does not use the preflight checklist to learn how to do something. She uses it because it will remind her of everything that needs to happen to ensure the flight is safe and predictable.

Checklists allow the pilot to be well prepared ahead of time with the information they will need to make good aeronautical decisions—that is to perform the work they are uniquely suited for, flying a plane. (See Figure 4.1.) They also allow the pilot to go over key functionality after the flight has ended. If a pilot waits until the craft is airborne to check on or deal with the myriad details of the flight, the workload may distract her from more critical priorities, or she may lack information that would have been easily available to her on the ground. Either case could lead to poor aeronautical decision making and result in a crash or near-miss event.

For decades now, pilots from civil, commercial, and military aviation have used a preflight checklist before every flight—a practice meticulously and universally woven into the laws and mores of aviation. The preflight checklist had its origin in 1935 at Wright Field in Dayton, Ohio. (With thanks for this research to John Schamel, a Federal Aviation Administration flight instructor and historian who has documented the rise of modern aviation.) Boeing had submitted its prototype for a long-range bomber to the U.S. Army Air Corps, the Model 299; it would be tested with prototypes from Martin and Douglas. The Boeing entry had swept all the Army Air Corps evaluations and was expected to win a major contract for between 185 and 220 aircraft.

The day had arrived for the formal flight testing on the airfields of Dayton. Army pilots Ployer Hill and Donald Putt would fly the plane, joined by Boeing's chief test pilot, Leslie Tower, Boeing mechanic C. W. Benton, and Henry Igo of Pratt-Whitney, the engine manufacturer. The massive bomber made a smooth takeoff but shortly thereafter stalled, wheeled, and crashed to the earth, bursting into flames to the horror of the observers. Putt, Benton, and Igo were able to run from the wreckage, though they were seriously burned. Hill and Tower were trapped inside but First Lieutenant Robert Giovannoli entered the burning bomber twice to pull out both men. These two men died of their wounds in the hospital, and unfortunately Giovannoli would perish soon thereafter in another airplane accident.

In the wake of the disastrous test, the investigation found that pilot Hill had neglected to release the elevator lock prior to takeoff. The crew evidently tried to fix their mistake as the plane began to ascend but couldn't reach the lock handle in time. It appeared that Boeing's prototype was doomed. Some in the media said the airplane was too complex and overwhelming. Because the prototype had excelled in

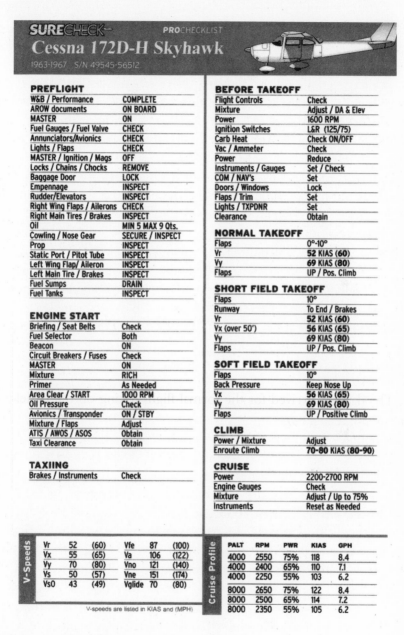

SURECHECK— *PRO*CHECKLIST
Cessna 172D-H Skyhawk
1963-1967   S/N 49545-56512

PREFLIGHT

W&B / Performance	COMPLETE
AROW documents	ON BOARD
MASTER	ON
Fuel Gauges / Fuel Valve	CHECK
Annunciators/Avionics	CHECK
Lights / Flaps	CHECK
MASTER / Ignition / Mags	OFF
Locks / Chains / Chocks	REMOVE
Baggage Door	LOCK
Empennage	INSPECT
Rudder/Elevators	INSPECT
Right Wing Flaps / Ailerons	CHECK
Right Main Tires / Brakes	INSPECT
Oil	MIN 5 MAX 9 Qts.
Cowling / Nose Gear	SECURE / INSPECT
Prop	INSPECT
Static Port / Pitot Tube	INSPECT
Left Wing Flap/ Aileron	INSPECT
Left Main Tire / Brakes	INSPECT
Fuel Sumps	DRAIN
Fuel Tanks	INSPECT

ENGINE START

Briefing / Seat Belts	Check
Fuel Selector	Both
Beacon	ON
Circuit Breakers / Fuses	Check
MASTER	ON
Mixture	RICH
Primer	As Needed
Area Clear / START	1000 RPM
Oil Pressure	Check
Avionics / Transponder	ON / STBY
Mixture / Flaps	Adjust
ATIS / AWOS / ASOS	Obtain
Taxi Clearance	Obtain

TAXIING

Brakes / Instruments	Check

BEFORE TAKEOFF

Flight Controls	Check
Mixture	Adjust / DA & Elev
Power	1600 RPM
Ignition Switches	L&R (125/75)
Carb Heat	Check ON/OFF
Vac / Ammeter	Check
Power	Reduce
Instruments / Gauges	Set / Check
COM / NAV's	Set
Doors / Windows	Lock
Flaps / Trim	Set
Lights / TXPDNR	Set
Clearance	Obtain

NORMAL TAKEOFF

Flaps	0°-10°
Vr	**52 KIAS (60)**
Vy	**69 KIAS (80)**
Flaps	UP / Pos. Climb

SHORT FIELD TAKEOFF

Flaps	10°
Runway	To End / Brakes
Vr	**52 KIAS (60)**
Vx (over 50')	**56 KIAS (65)**
Vy	**69 KIAS (80)**
Flaps	UP / Pos. Climb

SOFT FIELD TAKEOFF

Flaps	10°
Back Pressure	Keep Nose Up
Vx	**56 KIAS (65)**
Vy	**69 KIAS (80)**
Flaps	UP / Positive Climb

CLIMB

Power / Mixture	Adjust
Enroute Climb	**70-80** KIAS **(80-90)**

CRUISE

Power	2200-2700 RPM
Engine Gauges	Check
Mixture	Adjust / Up to 75%
Instruments	Reset as Needed

V-Speeds

Vr	52	(60)	Vfe	87	(100)
Vx	55	(65)	Va	106	(122)
Vy	70	(80)	Vno	121	(140)
Vs	50	(57)	Vne	151	(174)
Vs0	43	(49)	Vglide	70	(80)

V-speeds are listed in KIAS and (MPH)

Cruise Profile

PALT	RPM	PWR	KIAS	GPH
4000	2550	75%	118	8.4
4000	2400	65%	110	7.1
4000	2250	55%	103	6.2
8000	2650	75%	122	8.4
8000	2500	65%	114	7.2
8000	2350	55%	105	6.2

Figure 4.1   Preflight Checklist for a Cessna 172DH

Source: Reproduction courtesy of Sporty's Pilot Shop, Inc., www.sportys.com/PilotShop.

every other respect, Army Air Corps officers ordered 13 planes to keep the project alive. Boeing knew it was under intense military and congressional scrutiny. According to Schamel's account, "The pilots sat down and put their heads together. What was needed was some way of making sure that everything was done; that nothing was overlooked. What resulted was a pilot's checklist. Actually, four checklists were developed—takeoff, flight, before landing, after landing. The Model 299 was not 'too much airplane for one man to fly,' it was simply too complex for any one man's memory. These checklists for pilot and copilot would make sure nothing was forgotten."[1]

This tragedy not only resulted in the success of Model 299, which became the B-17, the most important bomber aircraft in American history, but instituted the preflight checklist, now in use for every commercial and private flight. The checklist is an inspiration for how liberated firms empower employees with confidence and insure from risk the successful daily flights we take each day for our clients. The characteristics of the preflight checklist transfer quite nicely to the professional services firm. The checklists and workflows assume each employee is trained and qualified, and are there to remove the stress of remembering every detail. The checklists are inclusive and can be modified and updated by each employee. The goal is that everyone in the company could follow the guidelines on a particular responsibility and achieve the same results. The liberated CEO's checklists are living, breathing documents that can be constantly changed and updated. It is a true gift to your employees and customers, because your staff is freed from the worries that they'll forget a routine step of an important process.

Because our brains tend to forget details when we are on information overload, removing the need to consciously focus on routine tasks frees each employee to do the productive, creative, customer-focused work that creates value and contented customers. It can also allow for a quick return to the task at hand after an interruption from a client phone call or e-mail. The true story of Model 299 also illustrates another key for managing people that the checklist delivers. Just as the pilot of the prototype bomber was not really at fault, but asked to fly a plane that was far more complex than previous craft, so it is that the preflight checklist allows us to isolate a problem with process rather than blame a person when that blame is not truly justified.

IRA to Roth Conversion Checklist

✓ Verify IRA is not a recent reconstitution

✓ Obtain conversion plan from Advisor

✓ Establish the Roth account(s) for the conversion if necessary

✓ Use this as an opportunity to verify beneficiaries are correct on both IRA and Roth accounts

✓ Prepare IRA conversion paperwork

✓ Obtain client signatures

✓ Forward paperwork to broker–dealer

✓ Verify that the conversion has happened

✓ Set evaluation follow-up task for end of November

Figure 4.2   Checklist Used in Navigoe—IRA to Roth Conversion

This is an example of one of a few checklists for the process of doing an IRA to Roth Conversion. This is one task as part of a larger workflow.

The checklist is part of a process each firm adapts to its own needs and client base. It can start with an owner's Excel spreadsheet where she writes down the steps of a core interaction, say, of preparing tax return information and documentation, or of the steps required to work with a lawyer on writing a will. The checklist becomes a joint document of your firm's operations and services. As a firm grows and adds staff, the checklists can be automated through software into automated workflows. (See Figure 4.2.)

AUTOMATED WORKFLOWS

The preflight checklist liberates your people to focus on their peak-zone work. The automated-workflow process uses a technology solution to embed your firm's checklists onto your CRM platform so that each step is prompted and recorded and accessible to all CRM users. In other words, workflow automation is a predefined, structured process where tasks representing the work required for each of the standardized steps in a process are automatically created and assigned to the right person at the right time based on business logic.

Automating workflows isn't really about automating the actual work people do. Rather, as observed by Crossvale CEO Conor Brankin, an expert in business process automation, the process reduces inefficiency and mistakes in the work handoff: "the work handoff between participants is a particularly inefficient, error-prone, and inconvenient boundary." Workflow automation is at its best performing these kinds of activities in an office, as noted by Brankin:

- Assigning steps of a business process to the appropriate person, and maintaining assignments—which team member performs a task.
- Notification—automatically notifies designated participants and observers, rather than relying on staff members remembering to send the e-mail, text, or fax.
- Task lists or checklists—as we said above, your checklists are integrated into workflow.
- Escalating tasks to a supervisor or manager—whether an error, missing a deadline, or exceeding a budget ceiling, automation can be programmed to reroute approvals or tasks based on triggers.
- Monitoring status of processes and projects—any manager or peer can check status without interrupting or distracting a colleague.
- Collecting metrics and audit logging—the system collects, stores, and assigns data for compliance and evaluation.[2]

In our business, the workflow records each employee's actions and communications including client notes, financial transactions, and requests. The automated workflow acts as the assembly line for client transactions, with your high-performing team members creating and distributing the financial, advisory, and intellectual products that are processed by this assembly line.

Navigoe has worked with My Virtual COO and other firms to embed automated workflows for common project transactions such as processing a client distribution. For example, the checklist for setting up a financial planning consultation was 18 to 25 steps long before automation, and 8 steps after automation. A series of eight steps involving research, preclient strategy meetings, and document writing are compressed into three by using Mind Maps and online client templates. The actual amount of data collected does not decrease, but an automated system orders the tasks among different employees in a more efficient matter. It allows employees to work at different speeds on items and only slows down one's next step if that person is waiting on another employee for completion of certain tasks.

By having this automated, all an employee needs to do is mark their task as completed, and the system will then assign the next task to the next person. Without an automated workflow, when you complete a task, you then need to notify the next employee that it is now time for them to do their task, in effect adding more steps. Also, at any time in the workflow, you can go into the workflow for a client and identify what has been completed, note the open items, and what items still need to be activated by the completion of an open item. If an employee is going to be sick for three days, others can go into the system and pick up the time-critical tasks for that employee, and in effect keep the process moving. CRM improves the transparency of team performance.

Of course, it does not take a computer program to monitor this process. However, one of the nice features of such a system is that it can be considered "set and forget." You do your work assignment, and you are not asked to do anything until the data is ready to be evaluated if waiting for someone else, for example. The practice of automating a process into a CRM system forces you to think through every step, its proper order, and who needs to complete the step. Then as you test the workflow as you designed it, you will quickly find out or be told if there is a problem with the process you've established. So while the implementation can take a little time, the net effect is much greater efficiency for everyone. You'll find your team will gain confidence, knowing they can rely on the system to walk a process throughout the office, rather than having to double check with an employee to track a process through multiple employees. (See Figure 4.3 for an example of an embedded workflow.)

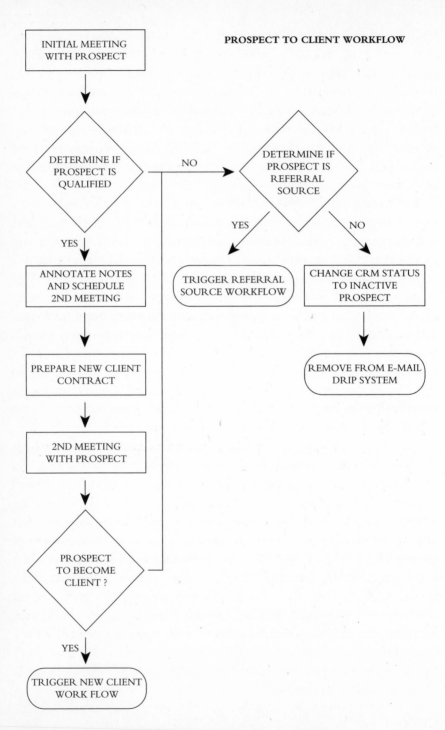

Figure 4.3   Sample Workflow Diagram Courtesy of My Virtual COO

SET IT AND FORGET IT

I've found the set-it-and-forget-it aspect is particularly valuable in terms of managing stress and staying focused on the best parts of the business. You don't wake up worrying about what you are missing or forgot to do. As a Quick-Start type, that was always my middle-of-the-night worry. I believed I was generally doing a great job for my clients, but feared that I was missing or forgetting to dot some *i* or cross some *t* that could have real implications. Naturally, as you add staff and clients in the early growth stages of your practice or business, you are adding tasks and complexity to your office processes. The cognitive effort required to oversee these myriad decision and transition points is substantial; the drain on your energy becomes part of the service ceiling we've discussed.

Set it and forget it has another benefit when it comes to delivering great customer service and pushing past the service ceiling. If you and other team members are interrupted for important client business, and if it kills the rest of your day, you can pick up exactly where you left off since the system shows you just where your work was interrupted. Automated workflows can make a virtue of multitasking by allowing you to have many balls in the air at one time and not feel too overwhelmed, especially when there are multiple-employee steps. You hand off assignments to the next person and move on with your next set of tasks, rather than waiting around for the response or reply.

Look, we know it's hard to invest in technology and intimidating to find the time to collect, record, and program all the historical data for business processes. Liberated firms don't do this for your own convenience, for the regulators, or because it's cool (although these are important too!). You do it for your people, so each member of your team can do what they do best, freed from the exhausting double-checking of transitional tasks and routine but crucial administration and project-management details. "By automating through integrated technologies," Jennifer Goldman said, "owners are helping their outsourcers and onsite staff to work at their highest and best use as much as possible and to have the time to share their expertise with the company's clients."

Setting up workflows and checklists are another example of leveraging the experience of an outside firm that works with your industry.

Navigoe was not the first company in the financial services industry to want to automate our systems. We did try to design workflows and incorporate the checklists on our own, with much of the work falling on me. After a couple of months of internal meetings, and flip-chart paper taped all over the office, I realized I was operating in my dead zone, and needed some help. By outsourcing the process, we not only got the technical expertise of writing the workflows in our CRM, but the best-practices experience of all those who had gone before us to work through much of the process already.

I have found in our business that the discipline of checklists also taught us that employee mistakes can frequently be traced to a point where a process failed—not the person. Far too many people in business make serious missteps by calling out, penalizing, or demoting employees when a mistake is made. Some see business as a zero-sum game where someone must be blamed or you will be. If you turn the telescope around and view the process in place when the mistake or problem occurred, you'll see these situations in an entirely new perspective.

This is a relatively simple change to make as a leader. We need to recognize we have a psychological bias as observers to attribute blame to the person who makes a mistake or violates a norm, even before we consider what influences or reasons led to that action and even if we actually know what might have contributed to the problem. This happens when someone runs a stop light or is speeding and we instantly blame them as bad drivers when in fact the person may have had an emergency that contributed to their driving behavior. This also happens at work.

Social psychologists label this as *fundamental attribution error*, and researchers have documented the effects for decades. Edward Jones and Victor Harris performed a classic study in 1967 where participants read essays that opposed or supported the regime of Fidel Castro. Some of the participants in the study were told that the essayist had chosen to write the essay—that these were the writer's own beliefs—while other participants were told that the essayist had been directly ordered to write the essay by the teacher. While the psychologists expected to confirm that the reader-participants would easily distinguish between what people wrote and what they believed, in fact even when participants knew the essayists were *required* to write the pro-Castro essay they still rated those writers as pro-Castro.[3]

As noted behaviorist Daniel Gilbert wrote in *Speeding with Ned*, "participants knew perfectly well that the essay's content had been dictated by the debate coach, and yet something about the actor's behavior elicited correspondent inferences."[4] This fundamental attribution error was found in more experiments over the ensuing years. In one study, the test participants were given pro-Castro arguments and were told that one group writing the essay had their arms twisted the same way—and the participants still rated that group as actually holding pro-Castro views. In another test, the essay readers actually assigned the pro-Castro topic to people who didn't believe it, and the readers still rated them as pro-Castro. For a number of reasons, we have a tendency to blame or attribute the person who makes a mistake even if we knew they had no knowledge of their error or intended something else entirely.

We discovered in evaluating and discussing our own business, that time and again—in far more cases than we expected—mistakes occurred because the process was broken, not the employee. This holds true for every business. Liberated CEOs look to where the process failed rather than what went wrong in a single situation. By doing so, your business makes fewer mistakes in the long run. You shield blame from the individual; you create a culture where employees know they are allowed to make mistakes, and therefore stretch their performance to reach higher levels.

As we discuss in Chapter 7, "Keeping a Loyal Crew," it is critical that a culture of teamwork is fostered within the company. By having everyone focus on the process, rather than the employee, you drastically reduce situations where negative feelings around staffers not pulling their own weight can quickly degrade morale within the office. Mistakes become the problem of the company and as a result it is a company-wide solution that needs to be sought after. This also removes the defensive, "Yeah, but" culture of employees to one of a proactive, "How do we all solve this?" mindset common with owners and managers.

Hire the best, outsource the rest, and then give your inside and outside teams the checklists and workflows they can control and update to manage their work ecosystem. Do all this through an overriding focus on providing clients with the best possible service, and you'll be getting up every morning with a fire in your belly to get to the office.

GIVE YOUR CREW PREFLIGHT CHECKLISTS
KEYS TO THE CHAPTER

Checklists, automated workflows, and fully integrated CRM software are essential to liberating the CEO and her team, by routinizing as much non-client-facing and back-office work as possible and building in safeguards and accountability. It can start with an owner's Excel spreadsheet where she writes down the steps of a core interaction, say, of preparing tax return information and documentation, or of the steps required to work with a lawyer on writing a will. The checklist becomes a joint document of your firm's operations and services. As a firm grows and adds staff, the checklists can be automated through software into automated workflows. Ramping up these processes will take some time and money, but the benefits are worth it:

- Valued employees gain more time and peace of mind to work with clients and other critical tasks.
- Ease of compliance, bookkeeping, and administrative work.
- Access and transparency improves training and on-ramping for new staff.
- Easy-to-find mission and client-critical transactions.

NOTES

1. John Schamel, "How the Pilot's Checklist Came About," September 10, 2012, www.atchistory.org/History/checklst.htm.
2. Conor Brankin, "7 Key Activities Automated Workflows Automate," Crossvale blog, http://crossvale.com/blog/7-key-activities-automated-workflows-automate, accessed September 23, 2013.
3. Daniel Gilbert, "Speeding with Ned: A Personal View of the Correspondence Bias," in *Attribution and Social Interaction*, ed. J. M. Darly and J. Cooper (Washington, DC: APA Press, 1998).
4. Ibid.

CHAPTER 5

―――――――

HOW TO BUILD
A SERVICE BRAND
(IT'S NOT ABOUT YOU)

Everyone talks about customers. Liberated businesses make customer awareness part of the fabric of every employee's job, and liberated CEOs learn a distinction that has escaped the vast majority of people in business: Customer relationships are not the specialty or skill of a particular function or department. They dictate how each and every employee makes decisions.

That's why our concept is about more than just delivering great customer service. It is also about designing processes so your system is geared in every aspect to have the client look to the company as a service brand, rather than to an individual. This is *only* possible if the other items in the book are followed. This chapter ties together the threads we've discussed about developing a world-class service team of employees not burdened by repetitive duties that can be outsourced, who are compensated well, are supported by checklists to minimize mistakes, and are empowered by the organization to get client service delivered in a timely manner. And there's another key: the CEO, founders, principals, and top partners need to step back from their egos and any cultures of personality to develop the people and processes that shape a growing business.

How a business engages customers has many variations depending upon the nature and size of the business and the views of leadership. Small and medium-sized businesses typically need strong customer relationships to survive. Different businesses have different methods for interacting and understanding customers. They include some of these models:

- The *data-centric model* solicits customer feedback on services and products and provides that data to staff members to ensure and manage customers' satisfaction.
- The *experiential model* focuses on the quality of the customer experience at every touch point between the customer and the company and places a great deal of emphasis on studying customer reactions and behavior (Starbucks and Apple are examples of companies that organize business processes around customer experience).
- The *co-creative model* educates and empowers customers to use their ideas and suggestions to shape products and services (consider Nike's and Converse's programs to allow customers to design their own sneakers, or Build-A-Bear, where kids can design, dress, and create narratives for their toy bears).

We recommend that you draw on these approaches as needed to build a *customer-customized* model—we advocate building customer awareness and training into every facet of business operations. We invest in changing everyone's behavior so the customer's needs are reflected in the moment-to-moment work routines of key employees. Customer service also should happen without drawing attention to itself, or customers will think you're looking for something in return; in the words of Cesar Ritz, who founded the Ritz-Carlton hotel chain, "people like to be served, but invisibly."

RULE #1

I admire Nordstrom's no-rules approach to meeting customers' needs. For many years, employees were given the *Nordstrom's Employee Handbook*, which turned out to be a single 5×8″ card containing these 75 words:

> **Welcome to Nordstrom**
>
> We're glad to have you with our Company. Our number one goal is to provide outstanding customer service. Set both your personal and professional goals high. We have great confidence in your ability to achieve them.
>
> **Nordstrom Rules: Rule #1: Use best judgment in all situations. There will be no additional rules.**
>
> Please feel free to ask your department manager, store manager, or division general manager any question at any time.
>
> During this time, Nordstrom had the highest sales per square foot performance in the retail industry—by almost double.
>
> *Source:* Matt Linderman, "37 Signals," http://37signals.com/svn/posts/2632-nordstroms-employee-handbook-mdash-short-and-sweet.

We share the view of Nordstrom department stores that customer service is a value everyone needs to own from the time they are hired and is one area where checklists and protocols are secondary. With the success of Nordstrom capped by Robert Spector and Patrick McCarthy's bestselling book *The Nordstrom Way*, published in 1996, businesses of every kind strive to call themselves the Nordstrom of their industry. This passage from the book is a call to action for every professional service firm:

> First and foremost, Nordstrom follows a strategy built around the customer—not around price, process, brand, technology, or any other corporate tactic or buzzword you can think of. When the company considers how it can improve service and results, it asks itself one question: "What would the customer want?"
>
> Everything Nordstrom does, every aspect of its business, is seen through the lens of the customer, with the goal of improving the experience that a customer has with Nordstrom. If it matters to the customer, doing it well is good customer service. That's why customer service is the number one priority. That's why the focus on the customer is emphasized and reemphasized and reemphasized at each and every opportunity. . .[1]

I also greatly admire the customer-service philosophy found in what some would say is an unusual place, the independently owned Texas de Brazil restaurant chain. In its own way, Texas de Brazil breaks the service ceiling of the food-service industry. They do this through non-stop training and communications, a focus on the customer's expectations, and a strong culture of promoting from within; as you can see, this framework doesn't just work for professional services firms.

Of course concierge services are easier to implement for a professional services business with high-net-worth customers. We'll show you how this model works in other industries as well.

In our business, I've documented the implications of having every staff member know our customers as individuals down to every detail of their relationship with the business. We train folks to help customers when it makes sense, not when the rules tell them to do so. Our business benefits include a better customer experience, a stronger emotional attachment to the firm, superior customer retention, higher customer loyalty, and therefore greater referrals.

Every liberated CEO needs to know a few principles of customer behavior. First, a satisfied customer is more likely to move his or her business than a *loyal* customer: Satisfaction is necessary to achieve loyalty but it is not enough on its own. Second, customer loyalty is both developed and tested by time: The longer you have a customer, the deeper the relationship, but the greater the chance that customer will

---

THIS PASSAGE FROM *THE NORDSTROM WAY* IS A CALL TO ACTION FOR EVERY PROFESSIONAL SERVICE FIRM

First and foremost, Nordstrom follows a strategy built around the customer—not around price, process, brand, technology, or any other corporate tactic or buzzword you can think of. When the company considers how it can improve service and results, it asks itself one question: "What would the customer want?

Everything Nordstrom does, every aspect of its business, is seen through the lens of the customer, with the goal of improving the experience that a customer has with Nordstrom. If it matters to the customer, doing it well is good customer service. That's why customer service is the number one priority. That's why the focus on the customer is emphasized and reemphasized and reemphasized at each and every opportunity . . .[2]

have a bad experience that tests her loyalty. Third, the stakes of customer satisfaction are high. Dissatisfied customers spread the word quickly and through the Internet they can vent their feelings with thousands of others. Fourth, loyalty or retention builds with consistent satisfaction, and research shows that customers experience satisfaction with a range of intensity levels. The more intensely loyal a customer is, the more referrals and more positive word of mouth he or she will generate.

In fact, satisfied customers or clients who recommend a business to others experience a higher level of emotional commitment to that business; word-of-mouth referrals have a double dividend for your business, according to a study done by Ina Garnefield, Sabrina Helm, and Andreas Eggert. By encouraging satisfied customers to spread the word, you increase their own willingness to remain with you.[3]

At the global car rental giant, Enterprise Rent-A-Car, CEO Andy Taylor responded to the challenges of rapid growth by developing detailed customer behavior surveys including live phone interview data. Enterprise discovered that completely satisfied customers were three times more likely to remain loyal than somewhat satisfied customers, even if they experienced an occasional, significant breakdown in service.[4] Noted Gallup researchers John Fleming and Jim Asplundh (as published in their book *Human Sigma* and articles in the *Gallup Business Journal*) found that financial services customers (and those in other industries) who describe themselves as extremely satisfied can be divided into two cohorts: those that have an emotional bond to the firm, and those with a cooler, rational view that they are satisfied.

These emotionally satisfied customers buy more products, spend more, return more often, and stay longer with the business. "Merely satisfying customers by delivering on their rational requirements represents a minimum point of entry for today's businesses; managing to satisfy customers will not drive the enhanced financial performance today's business leaders seek," Asplundh and Fleming wrote:

> To build the strong customer connections that produce enhanced financial benefits, a more complete view of customer requirements is needed, which incorporates an understanding of the emotional dimensions of customer commitment. Customers want more than transactions—they want relationships.[5]

This accurately describes the thinking behind our high-touch process. We build relationships by providing services that satisfy our customers' needs, but we also deliver emotional benefits, such as peace of mind and pride of stewardship, by exceeding expectations. Five exceptional factors shape our customer-service culture:

1. Hiring the right people.
2. Empowering them to help the customer.
3. Embracing disruption.
4. Anticipating and closing customer loops.
5. Sweating the small stuff.

HOW A BRAZILIAN RESTAURANT BRAND BREAKS THROUGH THE SERVICE CEILING

Source: Photo by permission of Anil Sekhri and Texas de Brazil.

The service ceiling in the restaurant business is shaped by factors including high employee turnover, the need for on the job training, and a super-competitive market. Breaking through the ceiling is about meeting and exceeding expectations night after night. Restaurant owners know that maintaining seamless, high-touch service and great food quality are the keys to customers' loyalty: They remove customers' doubt from the decision to invest in an expensive dining experience and build relationships. Achieving this standard requires sustaining a mindset and teaching a multitude of details among numerous employees on different shifts and, for chain restaurants, at various locations.

I have long studied the processes and culture of Texas de Brazil, a Brazilian *churrascaria* restaurant chain that stands above the competition in its service consistency and dining quality. In researching Texas de Brazil (TdB), I discovered that intense training, a passion for anticipating guest needs, frequent communication, and a promote-from-within policy, combine to create the amazing culture at TdB. Here are some highlights from a conversation we had with TdB's Director of Operations, Anil Sekhri:

What is the ownership of Texas de Brazil?

Everything in the United States is under direct control of the ownership group. We have 27 restaurants that we own, direct, and manage here in the United States. We franchise in overseas locations, and we are extremely selective in who we select as franchise partners. They need to have a long track record of restaurant management.

What type of experience do you want to deliver at Texas de Brazil?

We want to exceed our guests' expectations, and ensure that when they come into our restaurant they'll have many reasons to return. We teach the following: We are extremely grateful for every guest of Texas de Brazil. I talk to our general managers and remind them and their teams that the guests are the boss. The guests pay everyone's paychecks, and our responsibility is to anticipate their needs seamlessly and quietly.

The *churascurro* tradition is rooted deeply in Brazilian culture and passed down through the generations. It is a revered tradition and we want our guests to enjoy it without distractions.

What is your philosophy regarding customer service?

We train our people constantly to look at the dining experience from the customer's point of view. This is the food-service industry. We're not scientists. We're not inventing anything. We're taking care of people. We

(continued)

break our philosophy down to the simplest, fundamental idea: Take care of people how you want to be taken care of when you go out. A guest can feel the body language immediately if you're uncomfortable or annoyed with a guest's situation. If a guest walks in ten minutes before closing, they should have the same service experience they have at 6:00 P.M. Every general manager has internalized this credo.

What are the keys to your world-class service culture?

We never stop training, we believe in continuous feedback, and we promote from within and reward our employees. Our general managers teach every aspect of the fine dining experience, from how you walk a guest to their table, to how you present the wine list, to handling customer complaints. I am reviewing and checking in on restaurant operations every day, monitoring sales and costs among other data, and holding conference calls with general managers. I teach our GMs and managers to give feedback nightly. They need to be communicating and guiding real-time on the restaurant floor, like a sports coach. If an employee's doing something well, let them know; if an employee needs to make an adjustment, don't wait to talk to them; if someone really needs more training, get it. Nearly all of our GMs and senior managers were promoted from within; we move people up, and this is so important for us. It gives everyone on our team powerful reasons to buy into our coaching and training approach.

HIRING THE RIGHT PEOPLE

I've talked about the power of knowing people's strengths (in our case we like to talk about "their Kolbe"), and evaluating hires who will be working with customers for their social and communicative aptitudes and abilities. I don't expect introspective programmers to have the intuitive judgment for handling customer concerns, but we do expect it from customer-facing staff because we've already made sure they enter the job with that strength. As Bruce Nordstrom said many times about training salespeople, "We don't train them. We leave the training to their parents."[6]

EMPOWERING PEOPLE TO HELP

I will never reprimand an employee for helping a customer, even if the decision was unorthodox. One reason we automate and document our core business processes in checklists is to free up our people mentally and from a time perspective to respond as needed to our customers. Great customer service needs to be "always on," and you can't program that mindset ahead of time.

Since we advise our clients on most of their financial-related issues, clients occasionally fail to differentiate what information may need to go to the tax accountant versus what may be appropriate for our firm. As a result, paperwork specific to completing a client tax return is often delivered to our office by the client. Our response is to scan the documents and provide the information to the clients' accountant. We don't bother the clients with this—we get it done.

We don't do this because it is part of our contractual services, but rather because at the time of the error, it is just more convenient for the client to have us handle getting the documents to the correct location. We also proactively provide our clients' accountants with the information associated with investments that is required to complete the tax returns. While systematizing and automating tasks are a core principle, when it comes to individual clients, however, you have to become comfortable with inefficiency.

Many years ago, we used to send out quarterly performance statements to our clients. This was the single largest interruption to our normal business activities. While it only happened every three months, it took almost two weeks of time to make sure all the data were correct, to create the reports, print them, sort and package them, and mail them to our clients. A few years before I left on my sailing trip, we decided to stop mailing our clients quarterly reports and rather make them available electronically. Setting up this system actually allowed us to provide consolidated account balances on a daily basis, and portfolio performance updates monthly—all available on demand for our clients. This was an improvement in customer service and improved efficiency within our own firm. However, not all our clients agreed that this was an improvement. Some of them, mainly the older, retired clients, were not used to going to the Internet for their information, and preferred to have paper statements mailed to their homes. Others, while happy to access their data electronically, liked having that piece of mail, as it reminded them to review the material at least quarterly. As a result, we did have some pushback from a small number of clients about moving to electronic statements.

As you could imagine, I did not want to have two sets of systems for our quarterly statements. In conversations with these clients, I was able to get them to agree to accept electronic statements. Over time, many of those clients have talked with others in our offices and expressed how much they really wanted paper statements. In large part due to our policy of customizing customer service, the staff started to send paper statements to this small number of clients, without ever telling me. Of course, I caught them red-handed one time, stuffing statements into envelopes. Ultimately, what could I say? They were doing what was necessary for that small group of clients to provide them with excellent service.

One of the lessons that I took away from this experience is that even though I meet with all our clients, there are times when they will express their displeasure to the staff rather than to me; having the staff empowered to address the displeasure is critical. I have also learned that at times I get too caught up in process, systems, and efficiencies, which can be detrimental to providing excellent service, which is in fact what we are here to do for our clients.

I think my role as the efficiency monitor is important in the business. Someone needs to have a relentless drive to force the changes, which can be disruptive and time-consuming to set up and establish. But it is also critical to have others in the organization know when it is time to make the exceptions.

At the Ritz-Carlton, employees are given a $2,000 a day budget (the equivalent of hotel resources) to delight customers, or make a situation right as the individual sees fit. According to Diane Oreck, vice president of Ritz-Carlton's Leadership Center, "We are saying to our employees, we trust you. We select the best talent. Just help the guest. We do a lot of training around empowerment."[7] At Texas de Brazil, wait staff are taught to adapt and be flexible in meeting guests' expectations and dealing with their concerns. "We do have policies and procedures in place for dealing with customer complaints," Anil Sekhri told us. "But it is essential that we give staff flexibility to work outside of the parameters, as long as they generally make the right decision. We know there are times only the staff on the floor knows what it takes to have guests leave our restaurant feeling that their experience was positive. For example, when we have coupon programs discounting our prices, the coupon may be valid for eight people, but ten people show up. Our team has the freedom to allow the extra guests and then fill them in on the issue so they know for next time."

EMBRACING DISRUPTION

The biggest threat to customer satisfaction is passive avoidance. In professional services firms, retail businesses, and even larger companies, the unplanned questions and concerns of the typical customer often represent a distraction and interruption of a day's workflow for many professionals. Customers are people, and when people are treated in a way that makes them feel small or invisible they begin to feel threatened and their satisfaction plummets. In many cases, the customer's concern will not align with your urgent priorities—but indeed it will be more important.

We embrace disruption for those reasons. By responding to clients' concerns whenever they occur, we exceed their expectations. This builds a strong customer bond. Our philosophy is this: Nothing you are doing is more important than dealing with that client interruption, ever.

We close the loop on the customer's request or question with as few pass-arounds and callbacks as possible. As we have discussed in previous chapters, our staff are trained with checklists that teach them a great deal about how we operate, so they can address many types of questions. Here's our process for addressing client calls and queries:

- First of all, we do not have a receptionist. In the classic sense, a receptionist's job for an incoming phone call is to pass that caller on to someone else. Many times, the caller has to start telling their story to the receptionist so that they can be transferred to the correct extension, only to have to tell the story over again; or the client just asks to be transferred to an individual and hopes they do not get voice mail or that they are in fact asking to talk to the correct person. Neither of these scenarios is great for high-touch customer service.

- When the phone rings in our offices, for the first few rings, it is the job of any and all of the administrative assistants to answer the phone. After a few rings anyone in the office is empowered to answer the call; if the caller is a customer, each staffer is given the leverage to answer the question if that question is routine to look up or common knowledge. The goal is twofold: First, get the client the correct answer to their question in as short a period of time as possible, which may mean that the question is noted so that a return caller can have the answer. Second, it gets the clients used to looking to the entire organization as being able to address their questions, not a specific employee of the organization.
- If the client wants to talk to me or a partner, the phone answerer will determine the nature of the request and see if another team member can help immediately (if the principal is not available). Many of these calls are from long-term clients who may want to talk to me out of habit; by institutionalizing our approach, clients begin to look to the firm as a *service brand*, not just me or another principal.
- If the customer has a more complex or more involved request, such as an investment allocation recommendation, a call back may be necessary; naturally there are dozens of times a year I stay late at the office to reach out regarding an urgent or delicate customer question. Over time, however, we found that roughly 9 times out of 10 when a customer who initially asked to talk to a principal, another member of the staff could address their concerns without a callback. The best evidence of how this works is anecdotal, but most of the time clients no longer ask to speak with a principal, but rather go directly into their question or request with the person who answers the phone. They have learned to trust our judgment as to who can best address their important issue at hand.

Certainly, having almost every phone in the office ring with incoming calls is not the best use of everyone's time. It is an interruption and inefficient. That is why many firms hire a receptionist, or worse a computerized system, to route calls. But great customer service cannot start by wasting five minutes of a client's time as they figure out with whom they should be talking in an organization, or making them wait for a callback from a voice message they left when others in the company could have provided the answer on the spot. Great customer service is many times uneconomical. That is why it is so critical to be as efficient as possible, when appropriate, so that client interruptions are not viewed as interruptions but rather as the opportunity to do what our clients have hired us to do—provide great service.

As we discussed in the outsourcing chapter, just because it is possible to outsource a task or function does not mean that you should! Way too many self-proclaimed business gurus stress the need to be efficient, systemize processes, automate functions, and outsource, outsource, outsource. While I agree that these are all very important goals in building a great business, they cannot be pursued at the expense of the clients' experience.

I talked in the introduction about how my business has continued to grow while I was on my two-and-a-half-year sailing trip. That growth was purely from referrals from current clients. That only happened because our clients look to our firm as the provider of their satisfaction, not just me. It is one thing for long-time clients to allow me some time away from the office with my family. But it is a completely different level of trust and confidence for these same clients to refer our firm to their friends and family knowing that I would not be in the office for months at a time.

This authentic, personal consistency of service creates a strong trust attachment to the company. Customers are able to judge that the behavior they are witnessing isn't scripted, and so is coming from a genuine belief on the part of the employee. The Nordstrom's salesperson will always answer another question. The Zappos' representative will stay on the call to ensure your customer experience is positive. The Texas de Brazil host will welcome you to the restaurant even if it is 10 minutes before closing.

I've learned from sports how a true team culture can beat the star-with-a-supporting-cast culture. When I started coaching my kids' water polo team, a 10-and-under team, we spent a good amount of time working on fundamentals and team play. Then we entered a tournament and got clobbered by a team that had a superstar. When playing at UCLA and on the USA Team, we were all superstars, as were all the players on all the teams we played (obviously there were some super-superstars); I had forgotten about the issue of dealing with one player. So I taught our team how to deal with removing one or two players from the equation, and forcing the team to play as a team. By the time we entered a big tournament about six months after that first tournament, we won a major tournament. We did it with teamwork. The other top teams all had a superstar, and once we removed him from the equation—as best we could—they did not know what to do. The other teams were used to watching the superstar. Also, they were not used to playing a true team, where the scoring was well distributed among the players.

Many businesses are created by superstar entrepreneurs. However, to become liberated, that superstar needs to be able to put aside ego and praise for themselves, and build a team that in the clients' eyes are all stars. I cannot think of any championship team that was successful due to a single superstar. In fact, the best teams have multiple superstars and to win at the highest levels they have learned to leave their egos in the locker room and work together.

ANTICIPATING AND CLOSING THE CUSTOMER'S LOOPS

This perspective is critical to businesses that provide complex legal, financial, or management services—and in many other circumstances as well. In managing a multifaceted professional service, there are often downstream tasks relating to compliance, accounting, regulation, or just plain common sense that many firms leave open and unfinished unless the client or third party complains. World-class customer service requires considering the life cycle of the particular service offered and closing every potential loop. You need to anticipate what your customers need over the long term, or it's likely they'll find a reason to go somewhere else. As the famous Wayne Gretzky quote reminds us, "A good hockey player plays where the puck is. A great hockey player plays where the puck is going to be."

You may hire a law firm or online service to incorporate your firm—and they'll overlook telling you that you need to re-register your LLC with the state every two years. A law firm may set up incorporated trust agreements that require a number of compliance steps such as establishing a board of directors—and we've found that the busy partner may overlook or find it inconvenient to explain and follow through on these fine print issues that often are not a priority for the IRS but can become a problem when noticed. Many financial service firms will allocate your investments during your initial meetings and rarely give you more than a cursory annual call to discuss how to reallocate or change strategy in the context of economic cycles and events. Management consultants notoriously spend months analyzing a business client's operations, workforce, and market needs; they develop a sophisticated strategy and a 100-page PowerPoint, hand it over, and then move on to the next client. Even if the contract has expired, imagine the client's delight and gratitude if that management consultant had a process for working with the client twice a year to evaluate implementation and execution.

Anticipating client needs is also a game changer for retail and e-commerce firms. Online shoe retailer Zappos.com is justifiably admired for its anticipation of customer experience. Zappos reflects a key insight into selling footwear. If you buy online, you can never know whether a shoe fits. So Zappos offers free shipping and returns in anticipation of customer anxiety. Nike famously anticipated the lifestyle trend of listening to music in all forms of exercise and added a sensor to its sneakers that would collect data through the runner's iPod and make it available on a Nike+ website where runners can track their times, share progress, compete asynchronously, create charts, and deepen their running experience.

At Texas de Brazil, operations director Sekhri emphasizes how important it is to anticipate what guests need: "We've studied what customers expect from a fine-dining experience. Although our cuisine requires a degree of self-service, in every other way we train and retrain at a fine dining standard, and we know what our guests will be concerned about, from getting to the restroom to picking the right wine at the right price. When you truly anticipate their needs, they barely know you're taking care of them; it's seamless."

We anticipate and close loops with every customer. This requires knowing each person's life and professional circumstances, and incorporating those factors in annual or twice-a-year summit meetings where we go over current and long-term decisions connected to estates, trusts, wills, investment strategy, or personal matters such as divorces or deaths in the family. While this is commonplace now, we were early adopters of making all our clients' accounts and investment information available online—and we knew this was important by talking to our clients about how they used information. A recent issue of our newsletter addressed in detail all the challenges associated with estate planning, investment accounts, and digital financial data, where passwords are kept in secret and then unavailable to an estate after the individual passes away. Few firms are looking this closely at this issue. By maintaining this prospective service commitment with established clients, we are able to reinforce our value, refresh our bond, and re-demonstrate our mastery of their financial situation.

A powerful example of this lies in how we at Navigoe respond to a difficult life experience of a client, and find ways to learn from that experience to help current and future clients minimize similar eventualities in the future. One example of this occurred earlier in the 2000s, when a whole new set of privacy laws were set up, called HIPAA (The Health Insurance Portability and Accountability Act of 1996 Privacy, Security and Breach Notification Rules). Some of the new rules eliminated a hospital's ability to share information about a patient; for example, a major provision protected the privacy of any-one 18 years of age or older. Not long after these laws came into effect, a college student driving home from university got into a car accident. The parents (our clients) were unable to get any information or help make medical decisions for their child, since the child was over 18.

However, we believed—and I'm sure many would agree—that par-ents are very involved in the lives of their kids after they turn 18, and many of these young adults would want their parents' help in a medi-cal emergency, particularly before they were married or in a com-mitted relationship. By learning from this event, for every client with children over the age of 18, we now help establish medical powers of attorney for their now-adult children. This is really a legal issue and obviously not one typically provided by a financial services firm. But since we know this could be a circumstance that has serious repercus-sions for our clients and their families, and we know the ages of our clients' children and grandchildren, it made sense for us to go this extra mile for the very unlikely event it became an issue for a client.

At Navigoe, we have a retention rate of over 98 percent. We feel this is due to all the added tasks and services we provide for our clients. When we talk with our clients and ask them what we provide to them, most of the comments are some form of us providing peace of mind. The peace of mind is that someone is helping them to manage all the complex tax, estate, and investment strategies they have put in place. It is also about how they are better prepared for life's unexpected events. Ultimately, we are compensated as investment managers, and most new clients come to us with an investment concern. However, we believe all the extra services we provide help us acquire and keep our clients. Our high retention rate has not occurred by accident, but by careful design and consideration of the potential needs of our clients. By automating these processes, we are better able to provide the knowledge and services to each and every one of our clients.

Ask yourself: What services have I provided to my customers that have open loops in the future and do I want my clients to be surprised?

SWEATING THE SMALL STUFF

In our digitally accelerated, mobile communications environment, the elements of personal brand image and presentation can be overlooked in businesses that don't have a steady stream of customers entering their location. Many professional service firms invest in office space and stationery, lease some furniture that looks like it was stolen from the set of *The Office*, and thereafter lose their focus on their personal brand image. When you're in the middle of your business every day, you stop seeing your environment the way others see it; and let's face it, the vast majority of our communications are by e-mail. The computer screen seems to be the portal to your office universe. But that's not how others see it. Customers see your sterile or messy conference rooms; they see the typos slip into written communications; they notice when the brochures become laughably outdated; or that someone forgot to update the staff list on your website. Every customer whether consciously or subconsciously understands that attention to detail in your surroundings is a statement about attention to detail in your professional expertise.

Paying attention to particulars, from maintaining clean offices to error-free written communications, shows that you care about the customer because people know these standards require above-and-beyond effort. We know every time a customer visits Navigoe for a meeting that every inch of the office needs to be clean and that our conference room is welcoming and warm. We treat each e-mail as if it were a written letter of formal correspondence. Not in its length or tone, necessarily, but in attention to detail. Further, I'm convinced that setting these standards for quality lifts staff morale, reminds everyone that they work for a high-standards business, and that being associated with a dedicated team reflects favorably on each individual.

HOW TO BUILD A SERVICE BRAND KEYS TO THE CHAPTER

We can learn from a variety of successful customer-service philosophies, but liberated CEOs need to integrate client awareness and service into every facet of business operations. Clients must look to the firm for world-class service, not any single individual. Customer service is a value every staff employee needs to own from the time they are hired, and is one area where checklists and protocols are secondary. Among the retail brands we admire as models are Nordstrom department stores and Texas de Brazil, the Brazilian steakhouse chain. We offer five factors that form our customer service philosophy:

1. Hire the right people. To build a customer service brand, hire individuals who like and want to work with people if they are going to be working with customers.
2. Empower people to help the customer.
3. Embrace disruption. Client questions and concerns are going to be a distraction and interruption from other important work. Liberated businesses must acknowledge the conflict and help the customer anyway.
4. Anticipate and close customer loops. In managing a multifaceted professional service firm, there are often downstream tasks relating to compliance, accounting, filings, regulation, or just plain common sense that many firms leave open and unfinished unless the client or third party complains. World-class customer service requires considering the life cycle of the particular service offered and closing every potential loop.
5. Sweat the small stuff. Pay attention to details of your appearance, office, and formal communications to help attract and maintain customers.

NOTES

1. Robert Spector and Patrick D. McCarthy, *The Nordstrom Way* (Hoboken, NJ: John Wiley & Sons, 2012).
2. Ibid.
3. Ina Garnefield, Sabrina Helm, and Andreas Eggert, "Walk Your Talk: An Experimental Investigation of the Relationship Between Word of Mouth and Communicators' Loyalty," *Journal of Service Research* 14, no. 1 (2011): 93–107; *Strategy+Business*, May 27, 2011.
4. Andy Taylor, "Driving Customer Satisfaction," *Harvard Business Review*, July 2002, http://hbr.org/2002/07/driving-customer-satisfaction/ar/1.
5. John Fleming and Jim Asplundh, "Customer Satisfaction Is a Flawed Measure," *Gallup Business Journal*, September 13, 2007.
6. Matt Linderman, "37 Signals," http://37signals.com/svn/posts/2632-nordstroms-employee-handbook-mdash-short-and-sweet.
7. Ashley Furness, "The Secret to Ritz-Carlton's Service Mojo," Bill Quiseng blog, November 19, 2012, http://billquiseng.com/2012/11/19/ashley-furness-the-secret-to-ritz-carltons-customer-service-mojo/.

CHAPTER 6

BREAK THE SERVICE CEILING WITH SYSTEMATIC CUSTOMIZATION

This step had its roots in a visit to my doctor's office some years ago to find relief for a typical winter cold. My regular physician was out of the office, but her partner was able to deal with my sore throat and sniffles. Because I also have a medical history on file, namely high cholesterol and severe back pain from sport injuries, he was able to not only address the cold, but also consider my lifelong health needs. By looking at the top two pages of my chart, he realized that it had been a while since my last blood test, something that is important when taking statins for cholesterol. The time spent with the physician was less than five minutes, yet I was very satisfied with the service. That is when the light bulb went off in my head.

Whether right or wrong, under our current system, doctors need to see as many patients as they can. As a result, medical practices have become very efficient in leveraging the doctor's time. Nurses perform the initial intake, evaluate the vitals, and update records. After the visit with the doctor the office staff handles follow-up tasks, not the doctor.

The physician's office is not a great business inspiration in every way. But medical practices' patient management inspired me to develop what I call systematic customization—a potential breakthrough model for professional service and many small businesses.

After this doctor's visit, I set out to create our own medical-vitals worksheet for every client. Each customized worksheet has all the information we need to review, discuss, and propose solutions, with a detailed understanding of our clients' concerns and goals. Because we set repeatable procedures for everything by systematizing all our processes (except for customer engagement and service), we had the opportunity to make the client meeting far more productive than in the past, so that the entire session dealt with creating value and meeting the needs of the customer. I realized I'd discovered a wonderful improvement on our system—what I came to call systematic customization.

As you know by now, I am a big advocate for having solid processes and systems in your business. Some processes are implemented with checklists, others through a manual. Whenever possible, you automate routine services through customer relationship management (CRM) including outsourced services. By doing so, you ensure that the people you've hired, trained, and developed are devoted to the customers who generate life-giving income.

That principle played out when I was on my sailing trip and then returned to the office every quarter. Most of my time was spent in meetings with clients. We have four to five client meetings a day! That schedule sets the tone for a business like mine, where four to five full-on, comprehensive client meetings in a week would be considered a lot. Major client meetings require about a day's worth of preparation and research; systematized customization allows us to handle this workload with greater speed and efficiency. Why? Because we've created and updated a vitals worksheet for each client since they joined our firm, and when they come for their checkup we're not preparing for the meeting from scratch.

APPLYING THE VITALS WORKSHEET TO YOUR BUSINESS

Many of the processes we've discussed are reflected in your firm's versions of the medical vitals chart for every client. The vitals chart can work for high-volume retail businesses in terms of frequent, valued customers who should have their own worksheet/file. (Say you're a salon: Imagine the flexibility if you have updated, solid, vital information for your customers so if their beautician leaves, you possess detailed knowledge about each client's haircut and color, family information, timing between visits, and other preferences.)

TONY BUZAN'S SEVEN STEPS TO MAKING A MIND MAP

1. Start in the center of a blank page turned sideways. Why? Because starting in the center gives your brain freedom to spread out in all directions and to express itself more freely and naturally.

2. Use an image or picture for your central idea. Why? Because an image is worth a thousand words and helps you use your imagination. A central image is more interesting, keeps you focused, helps you concentrate, and gives your brain more of a buzz!

3. Use colors throughout. Why? Because colors are as exciting to your brain as are images. Color adds extra vibrancy and life to your Mind Map, adds tremendous energy to your creative thinking, and is fun!

4. Connect your main branches to the central image and connect your second- and third-level branches to the first and second levels, and so on. Why? Because your brain works by association. It likes to link two (or three, or four) things together. If you connect the branches, you will understand and remember a lot more easily.

5. Make your branches curved rather than straight-lined. Why? Because having nothing but straight lines is boring to your brain.

6. Use one key word per line. Why? Because single key words give your Mind Map more power and flexibility.

7. Use images throughout. Why? Because each image, like the central image, is also worth a thousand words. So if you have only 10 images in your Mind Map, it's already the equal of 10,000 words of notes!

Source: www.tonybuzan.com/about/mind-mapping.

The worksheets are particularly useful for meetings where you present your plan for new business, or new strategies—those uniquely valuable offerings that set your firm apart from the competition. For many professional service firms, the make or break time for your business's success is the client meeting where you present a key deliverable to your clients. This could be a new floor plan in interior home design, a financing strategy for a real estate transaction, a retirement plan in financial services, a new blueprint in architecture, a detailed multigenerational estate plan in legal services, or a growth strategy in business consulting.

What makes the client meeting so critical is being prepared for the unexpected. The more comprehensive your services, the more difficult it becomes to stay on top of all the relevant information for each and every client. The more clients you have, the more this problem grows. This is in essence the service ceiling.

The ability to systematize the collection and retrieval of relevant information is critical to being able to deliver great services. It is the formal client meeting—and all that goes into the preparation and follow-up—that is the most difficult to systemize and as a result becomes a barrier to sustained progress.

At Navigoe, we provide wealth-management strategies and services built on a set of deeply researched, proven assumptions and approaches. For a particular client at a particular time, we address concerns that span from implementing an investment portfolio to managing tax strategies, to designing an estate plan or managing a business cycle downturn.

Any service firm will benefit from systematic customization. The more complicated the services, the more important is the need for you to systemize how you gather, organize, analyze, and ultimately deliver information to your client. Business consultants are an excellent example. They may need to assist and coordinate services among multiple legal firms, pension actuaries, accountants, and investment advisors. They will also advise on the hiring of new employees, developing job descriptions, evaluating outsourcing opportunities, and creating processes. They need to know as much about the big picture of the business as the owner, but they must have this level of intimate knowledge for all the business clients they serve.

For our client vitals worksheets at Navigoe, we use the Mind Map, originally developed by the legendary British educator, innovator, journalist, and management-thinking guru Tony Buzan.[1] Mind Mapping is a way to take and organize notes that helps the right and left sides of the brain work better together. We like how the Mind Map allows us to have a good deal of information on a single page. We print our Mind Maps in color on 11 × 17 paper. Aside from the meeting agenda, the Mind Map is the only item we physically present to our clients at our meetings. See Figures 6.1 and 6.2 for examples of Mind Maps.

Our Mind Maps capture critical information about the client that is necessary for us to answer most questions, including basics such as age, net worth, employment, family, goals, investments, real estate, insurance, and allied professionals. It also includes summaries or conclusions of more in-depth information taken from different programs, such as tax rates, retirement needs analysis, extended family tree, expenses, estate tax projections, charitable contributions, and family gifting. The final piece includes the open items being discussed and addressed on an ongoing basis.

It is not uncommon for us to have a two-hour meeting, exclusively to look at and address items on the map. We take all our notes during the meeting directly onto the map. After the meeting, the paper is handed to a staffer who will update the Mind Map with any changes and extract the required to-dos from the meeting. We assign the appropriate task in the client relationship management system to the employee who will be responsible, and finally send out a follow-up letter to the client summarizing our conclusions and action steps from the meeting, which helps to remind the client of any information we need them to provide.

Most of the preparation for the Mind Map is handled by the same employee who gets the Mind Map after the meeting. In our firm, that employee is gathering the information from six different pieces of software and consolidating it into the Mind Map. This process creates the agenda for the upcoming meeting, which is sent to the client in advance with a note reminding them of the meeting date, time, and location. All of this is being handled by employees and is very scalable as our firm grows.

Through this process, I can use my time with clients more efficiently. The best test of this has been when I would return to the office for meetings during my two-and-a-half-year sailing trip.

Typically, we will have four two-hour meetings scheduled a day. The day before the meetings, I review the maps with the whole office.

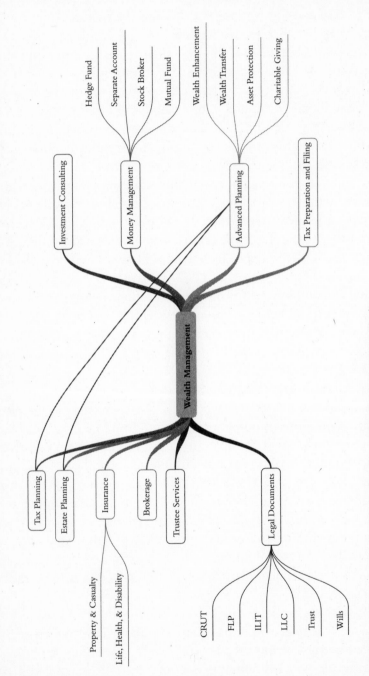

Figure 6.1 Scott's Overview of Navigoe's Wealth-Management Approach

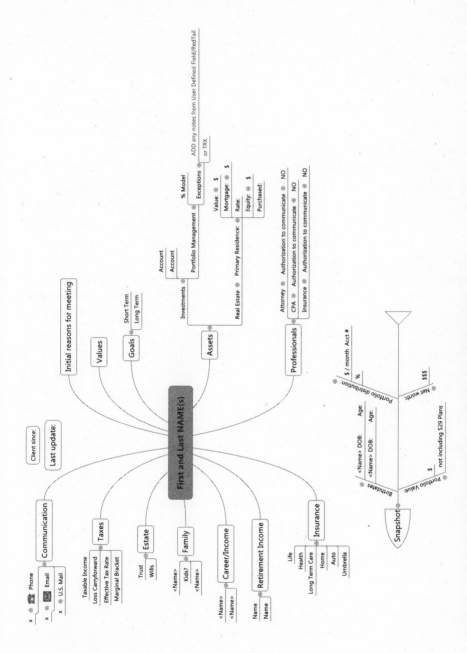

Figure 6.2 Navigoe's Template to Begin Each New Prospect Interview

It takes less than half an hour per client to perform the review, which allows me to get my head into the upcoming meetings for the next day, and to allow for any changes that may be necessary. On the day of the meetings, I need about five minutes to review the Mind Map before the client's meeting. After the meeting, it may take another five minutes to make sure that all the follow-up notes are correct and ready to go. Then I am off to the next meeting, free to focus on the next client knowing our client's needs from the previous meeting will be superbly handled. With this great process in place, I sleep much more soundly than the years before this system was in place.

This is systematic customization at work, and it has allowed me to leverage my time and perform in my peak zone for the company. It has increased the number of clients I can assist by an order of five. And ultimately, it was a key component that allowed me to continue to work on the business while sailing around the globe with my family.

Systematic customization works for department heads and many other functions in a business. If you're in a larger corporation as a marketing director, you can create vitals worksheets for different accounts you service, and suddenly you can have more productive meetings in less time, and easily work away from the office more frequently. A sales manager can create the same leverage with their accounts. This system easily translates to professional services such as real estate brokers, architects, accountants, and even engineers who are paid project fees.

So while every meeting with a client is a true, one-off custom event, with the Mind Map we have found a way to systematize the process. The key is to systematize your custom activities as much as possible. This won't happen overnight, and it may take some time to fine-tune the process. However, the results in your firm's efficiency will be surprising. Most importantly, it will probably even improve the excellent service your firm already provides.

Allow me a brief departure to address how I've handled communications and technology while sailing, as I've been able to interface and interact with all these systems worldwide ranging from the Bahamas to the South Pacific. A few years ago I stopped traveling with a laptop. I have desktop machines in all my offices, including home, work, and boat. But I have found that my iPad with a little external keyboard is much more useful than my laptop ever was.

One of the biggest reasons I prefer the iPad to a laptop is that the iPad is instant on and off, and it is easy to operate with one hand while being held with the other. All my iPad base-productivity programs— such as taking notes and accessing the calendar—are seamlessly coordinated with the office. Since most of the apps also sync with the iPhone, the data is almost always with me. I use the newsstand app to read *The Economist*, the *Wall Street Journal*, and sailing magazines.

You know by now how much I like Mind Maps. Rather than using the traditional notes app, I take all my notes, brainstorming, and middle-of-the-night ideas, on a mind map app called iThoughtsHD. It also should be no surprise I am one of those people who really likes to make to-do lists. I now use the app called ToDo by Appigo on my iPad and it syncs to my iPhone.

I have found it efficient to have multiple e-mail accounts. I actually have six different e-mail accounts that I access: three navigoe.com e-mails, one for clients, one I share with the world, and one that is private for employees. I also have three gmail.com addresses: my standard personal e-mail, a junk e-mail for when I am forced to give an e-mail address to access some website or for a hotel, and one for the boat/ sailing trip for use when we are just on the satellite. In a way, this helps me to triage the more than 200 e-mails I receive in any given day. Again, the efficiency of presorting e-mail into different buckets means I can give more focus to the e-mails from clients, staff, and friends.

CUSTOMIZATION IS SWEEPING KEY INDUSTRIES

Systematic customization works for both services and manufacturing. For service firms, customer interaction and value creation take place in singular, one-at-a-time experiences: Every client meeting is in effect a customized event. In manufacturing, processes must be, by necessity, systematic; the very essence of the assembly line. Firms from across the spectrum of service and manufacturing can merge these two concepts; we can point to excellent examples of firms and professions thriving as a result of either customizing their assembly line or systematizing their personal service.

I have already discussed the doctors' office. Their revenue model forced customized systemization upon them, which is largely controlled by the insurance industry. However, it is still a respected and highly compensated profession. The final step in this book talks about becoming active as a teacher and mentor in your industry. I have taught and coached many financial services firms about how to create and implement their own form of systematic customization, and in every single case it has improved productivity and client satisfaction.

On the manufacturing side, one of my favorite examples is Levi's jeans. They are not only a great story of systematic customization, but a classic business-school example of fostering innovation and change to keep an old brand vibrant and relevant. Levi's started making jeans for women in the late 1920s. They started as a work product, not a fashion statement. When all the designer jeans hit in the 1980s, Levi's had to evolve to stay relevant. Jeans became more about fashion than a practical, sturdy work uniform. Levis drove jeans fashion and market share with their button-fly design and alternative wash treatments when I attended high school in the 1980s. And they didn't stop there. They continued to innovate, drawing on a new strategy of systematic customization.

Clothing is generally made one of two ways: it is either systematic mass-production or customized, tailored one item at a time for a specific individual. However, in 2010, Levi's announced their Levi's Curve ID system. Up to that point, their jeans were sold based on the same two basic measurements: waist and inseam. Through extensive research, cost, and risk, Levi's decided to change the way they cut, fit, and sell their jeans to women. In thousands of retailers worldwide, women can go into a store and be measured by a fit specialist. (Read: customized service.) After this, the proper fitting jean can be selected for a woman based on her unique curves rather than just the length of her inseam.

This change was an enormous risk for Levi's as they had to have all the different cuts of jeans in the store for the initial rollout to be successful. They had to be willing to assume the gamble that in the growing age of Internet shopping, women would be willing to go into a store and have not just their waist, but their seat and hips, measured and recorded. At the end of the day, the jeans are all still mass-produced someplace. However, the process of finding a better way to size jeans allows for a more custom fit—and greater confidence among buyers. More important, Levi's expanded the mind share for their brand among women consumers.

Customization is one of the most transformative trends in the consumer economy. Look at Ford and the U.S. auto industry, which is booming. Henry Ford invented the assembly line early in the twentieth century, and Ford said of his pioneering Model T, "Any customer can have a car painted any color that he wants so long as it is black." Ford was one of the inventors of systemization and his success with the assembly line made much of what we know of the twentieth-century, Western-consumer capitalism possible. Today, you can custom make your Ford car online, choosing all manner of iterations from exterior color to interior color and fabric type, wheels, trim, stereo, and much more.

Consumers respond to the feeling that they are getting special treatment. It's human nature. We all feel we are unique and special, and want to be treated as such. Systematic customization empowers professional service firms to standardize many one-to-one standard business interactions while expanding opportunities for one-on-one customized service experiences; it also enables manufacturing businesses to deliver custom products and generate additional value from a one-to-many, assembly-line process. By using this principle, businesses of all types are deploying technology and communications to free creative entrepreneurs and executives to do what they do best.

Systematic customization should be applied to all situations where your firm has contact with its clients. In our firm, as with yours, most likely, customer e-mail has become a difficult beast. We pride ourselves on world-class service, but clients have reached the point where they expect responses to e-mail as if they're asking you a question live on the phone. They certainly do not want to spend the time figuring out who should receive the e-mail. Many times e-mail is the primary relationship contact for the client. What's more maddening is that most times the first-line recipient of the e-mail is not the person who is going to gather the necessary information for the reply. We all know how stressful managing customer e-mail can be.

Liberated CEOs do e-mail differently. And it works. E-mails should never go back to a client with an out-of-office notice. Clients are fine with the fact that people are not in the office all the time; however, if you think about it, any company dedicated to customer service should never leave the impression that no one is around to help a customer with an issue that needs to be addressed.

At Navigoe, we have solved these problems by giving all our clients a single e-mail address. (Since only clients know this very private e-mail address, this eliminates spam on this e-mail address, and therefore the problem of e-mails getting stuck in the spam filter.) All employees who work with clients have access to this e-mail account and read it frequently. All correspondence with the client happens through this single e-mail account. The benefits for the client are that they correspond with a single e-mail account with our firm and they never get an out-of-office notice. Also, our response time has drastically decreased as someone is almost always checking that account. The response may be a simple as, "We received the request and are doing some research, we'll get back with you." Last, it helps to further solidify the concept of Step Five, building a service brand.

LIBERATED CEOs DO E-MAIL DIFFERENTLY

In our firm, as with yours, most likely, customer e-mail has become a difficult beast. We pride ourselves on world-class service, but clients have reached the point where they expect responses to e-mail as if they're asking you a question live on the phone. They certainly do not want to spend the time figuring out who should receive the e-mail. Many times e-mail is the primary relationship contact for the client. What's even more maddening is that most times the first-line recipient of the e-mail is not the person who is going to gather the necessary information for the reply.

Liberated CEOs do e-mail differently. And it works. E-mails should never go back to a client with an out-of-office notice. Clients are fine with the fact that people are not in the office all the time; however, if you think about it, any company dedicated to customer service should never leave the impression that no one is around to help a customer with an issue that needs to be addressed.

At Navigoe, we have solved these problems by giving all our clients a single e-mail address. (Since only clients know this very private e-mail address, this eliminates spam on this e-mail address, and therefore the problem of e-mails getting stuck in the spam filter.) All employees who work with clients have access to this e-mail account and read it frequently. All correspondence with the clients happens through this single e-mail account. The benefits for the client are that they correspond with a single e-mail account with our firm and they never get an out-of-office notice. Also, our response time has drastically decreased as someone is almost always checking that account.

A major benefit to the firm is that it keeps all client correspondence open to be viewed by most people in the company. Anyone can go back and review an e-mail conversation with a client very quickly. It creates multiple eyes viewing the custom communications with clients. This creates checks and balances that help to ensure we continue to deliver excellent service around one client request.

This sounds counterintuitive to many people and certainly goes against the trend of outsourcing everything and only checking e-mail two times a week. The process has added an additional e-mail account for our employees to monitor. Systematic customization is about delivering a world-class experience for your client as opposed to maximizing employee efficiency at every opportunity. Having everyone answer client e-mails presupposes that the individuals on your team are highly motivated and share a sense of ownership and commitment to the firm. For more insight on fostering this culture in your organization, let's turn to the next chapter.

BREAK THE SERVICE CEILING WITH SYSTEMATIC CUSTOMIZATION KEYS TO THE CHAPTER

The role of patient charts in medicine inspired our breakthrough strategy for leveraging all the steps of *The Liberated CEO*. The result was we created our own medical-vitals worksheet for every client. Each client has their own well-documented file providing all the information we need to review, discuss, and propose services, with a detailed understanding of

(continued)

their concerns and goals. Our automated workflows and CRM platform are efficient in populating the core of the client worksheet from their files, which we then customize in meetings held before the client meeting. The result is a Mind Map, which includes our guidance and next steps focused on that particular client.

Major client meetings require about a day's worth of preparation and research; systematic customization allows us to handle this workload with greater speed and efficiency. The more comprehensive your services, the more difficult it becomes to stay on top of all the relevant information for each and every client. The more clients you have, the more the problem grows. The ability to systematize the collection and retrieval of the relevant information, on the fly, is critical to being able to deliver great services.

Any service firm will benefit from systematic customization.

NOTE

1. Tony Buzan, "What Is a Mind Map?" www.tonybuzan.com/about/mind-mapping/.

CHAPTER 7

KEEPING A LOYAL CREW

Numerous business owners have a problem they don't like to talk about. They tend to be embarrassed about it and hope it goes away without their bringing it out in the open. Many don't realize that far more people share this affliction than they suspect, and they continue to suffer in silence. It's a subject that even our most admired leaders find hard to articulate. Do you know what I'm talking about? It's managing your people. It's dealing with all the issues that arise from getting to know people as we do in the workplace. It's responding to the issues that arise as your people develop their own work relationships. As I've written earlier, many of us got into our own business because we like working with clients on our own terms and in our own style, and are pretty good at that. Translating our passion and vision to others can be a lot harder than it seems at first, and that's only an early step. We need to do more than communicate well; we must align our business goals, values, and leadership style with how we compensate and reward our staff. We need our crew oaring in the same direction and for the right reasons. Otherwise, the CEO will be stuck in the middle of the boat for far too long, trying to tell individuals when and how to row, rather than choosing the course for the boat to take.

The first step in pursuing change is admitting you have a problem, and when it comes to managing people and keeping a loyal crew, we should all just admit it is difficult and nowhere near as intuitive or commonsensical as it seemed when we started out in our business. If there's a secret ingredient to our success, and the success of many successfully liberated CEOs, it's this: Workplace culture is key and having each member of your team thinking like an owner is the foundation to culture. When done properly, the strategies outlined in this chapter and the next will help to change your company from a personal-service firm to a true business, with a long-term expectation of longevity beyond the founder.

What makes culture important? In a column by Josh Patrick, founder and principal of Stage 2 Planning Partners, published in the *New York Times' You're the Boss* blog,[1] Patrick wrote, "When I coach people on hiring, I always start with culture, which I define as what you value, what is important for you and your company. Culture always starts with the owner. In companies where culture is well defined, it is reflected in every hiring decision. But it can be complicated. I see problems when companies do not pay attention to the traits that make people successful in their companies. Do you want people to work independently, or do you think teamwork and collaboration are more important? Is working lots of hours essential? If you don't know the answer to these questions, you may have problems." The more you are successful in coaching and leading your team to share what you value and what is important for you, and in helping people change behavior to align with those values and priorities, the stronger your culture will be. As Josh says, it starts with the owner/principal. Culture may seem soft and vague to many, but ignore it at your peril. Without a commitment to a strong culture, you're likely to get stuck in the dead zone we spoke about in Chapter 3.

You know the acronym TLC (tender loving care); I am all for TLC, but the TLO mindset—Thinking Like an Owner—has changed the world. This mindset is one of the most productive and positive forces in the history of successful economies. The citizens of the United Kingdom re-elected Margaret Thatcher three times in large part because she gave working people the freedom to think like owners and act like owners because she supported and incentivized home ownership, cut taxes, and encouraged more market freedom and upward mobility. In the Silicon Valley technology sector, stock and business ownership in various forms was a driving force in attracting top researchers, engineers, and executives to startups that went on to change the world—and that remains the case. In fact, profit sharing as a powerful incentive is woven into the history of small businesses in the American economy.

Albert Gallatin, the Secretary of the Treasury under Presidents James Madison and Thomas Jefferson, advocated for profit-sharing programs as early as the 1790s. Gallatin introduced profit sharing at his glassworks company in New Geneva, Pennsylvania. Gallatin wrote, "The democratic principles on which this nation was founded should not be restricted to the political process, but should be applied to an industrial operation, as well."[2] Small businesses and family farms popularized the use of profit sharing during the eighteenth and nineteenth centuries as a supplement to limited on-hand cash, but it was not until the early 1900s that larger U.S. corporations began experimenting with and adopting profit sharing. Iconic companies such as Procter & Gamble; Eastman Kodak Company; Sears, Roebuck & Company; S.C. Johnson; and others became early adopters and maintained profit sharing for decades. Over time, financial and compensatory regulations changed and new options emerged for staking employees in their firms.[3] Options are still a major source of savings for millions of Americans. The iconic, historical home that we converted to the worldwide headquarters for Navigoe was purchased in large part from employee stock options that my wife accumulated while working for Oracle after college.

Many of the most admired, best companies to work for are majority employee-owned, such as W.L. Gore, Publix Supermarkets, King Arthur Flour, Autodesk, Principal Financial Group, Mrs. Fields Cookies, and Price Chopper stores. Small and service businesses can use various compensation approaches to help instill an ownership culture without a full-fledged stock option program. Respected academic research by Rutgers' labor economist Douglas Kruse and sociologist Joseph Blasi provides "extensive evidence" that employee ownership improves business performance. As they wrote in *Work in America*, "Broad employee ownership can result in better corporate performance over the long term. In general, empirical research using large samples of corporations and statistical controls suggests that broad-based employee ownership can result in one-time but sustainable increases in total shareholder return of 2 percentage points and productivity of 4 percentage points.

Some studies suggest that returns on equity go up by 14 percent, returns on assets go up by 11 percent. . . . A number of studies strongly suggest these effects are the result of combining employee ownership with a participatory and team-oriented culture."[4]

Profit sharing, owning shares of company stock, and other forms of economic ownership are important, but they are only one strategic aspect of building a TLO culture. We've preached world-class client service throughout this book, and we hold that your employees should be seen as clients of your business as well—because their values, attitudes, skills, and motivations are transmitted to those very clients who are so valuable.

THE VIRTUES OF THE TLO MINDSET

"Most advisors do not dream of the opportunity to recruit and manage people. They prefer to work with clients," said authors Mark Tibergien and Rebecca Pomering in their invaluable guide for financial advisors, *Practice Made (More) Perfect.* "But those who choose to grow their organizations and build their teams recognize that giving their staff the same attention they give clients can be just as valuable, if not more so. Creating a business that draws on more than just their own personal time and resources is how they discover the power of organizational leverage."[5] The virtues of the TLO mindset include reinforcing loyalty, aligning with core strategy, fortifying your business's values, sustaining your succession plan, and encouraging continuous learning.

A major focus of Chapter 7 is how critical it is that compensation provides key employees with a stake in ownership of a business. Let's remember that the principals of a firm also need to be compensated, and how that is done may be the ultimate measure of liberation (you can have one or multiple owners, of course, and not all of them may have employee responsibilities such as CEO). The next chapter will speak to various options for how firm ownership and profit allocation supports CEO succession and the selling of the firm for maximum value. Only by setting up the business so it has the highest value to a potential buyer will the CEO be ultimately liberated. If a business loses value at sale because the founder/CEO is leaving, he has failed because he has made the firm's success too reliant upon his own skills and charisma. That, too, is part of thinking like an owner!

Developing a TLO mindset in your business means:

- Viewing employees as assets, like clients, not liabilities like computer equipment.
- Communicating the big picture.
- Fixing the process before you blame the people.
- Linking compensation to the appropriate performance.
- Managing culture through participation, training, and transparency.

Let's briefly review how each of these play out in a business.

VIEWING EMPLOYEES AS ASSETS LIKE CLIENTS, NOT LIABILITIES

The fresh-horses syndrome is common to the growth (and failure) of many professional services businesses. As your business enjoys early success, you're having fun (you're working in your peak zone). You're doing a superb job for a handful of clients who appreciate your skills. You haven't yet expanded beyond the need for one or two employees whom you've known and worked with for a number of years. Your team doesn't require a lot of managing, and when one or the other key employees has a work–life issue or needs to change some aspect of their job, you don't want to add staff and costs so you give them flexibility, and the other members of your business family work more hours to cover the situation. You like having the small team that doesn't need a lot of formal bureaucracy. Performance reviews feel cold and corporate. Most owners don't analyze what's happening, but you're doing what's easy. You're relying on people who don't need much of your time or guidance. Founder-managers will favor those people who started with them and have already self-selected as trustworthy colleagues who are accountable and motivated.

As you continue to succeed, you begin to hit the service ceiling. You're getting referrals and clients who've heard about what a wonderful advisor, lawyer, consultant, or public relations guru you are. You need to hire people you hope are as good as your start-up team. But as an entrepreneur you're not necessarily inclined to instill onboarding, training, and review processes. You're hoping they'll be like the people you already have. The result? You keep using the employees who meet your expectations and stop relying on anyone as soon as they don't. People are let go and new people are hired. Or worse, your commitment to your people makes it very difficult to fire only the worse employees, so you slog through with a less than ideal crew. Your clients know the difference—you're not the start-up you used to be. You're stuck in the dead zone.

This is a familiar cycle. You know the skills and qualifications you need and you can screen, interview, and hire folks who have them. But then what? If they don't get it on their own, and self-manage their way to success, they begin to disappoint you and you go to them less. And, the horses who do their jobs well begin to fatigue because you're relying on them to do more than their share—leading to dissatisfaction and resentment.

If you continue with this pattern your stalwarts may leave you. What's the counterproductive mindset at the core of this behavior? It's that an employee is a cost center in whom you can't afford to invest time and resources—who soon becomes like a used car with too many miles. Tibergien and Pomering pinpoint the failure: "For years now, advisors have been lamenting the difficulty of finding good people," they note. "How odd that is, considering the number of qualified people looking for jobs. Are the people you interviewed and hired really not talented or hardworking, or are they being mismanaged?"[6]

Unconsciously, so many managers view employees as liabilities because they pay them, and fear the unknown costs of investing in them. But building a business by finding the one employee out of ten qualified ones who doesn't need support, systems, and training is an impossible algorithm. Do you want to turn your practice into a business that sustains your clients and their satisfaction as the source of value? Then you need to sustain those very employees who work with your clients and provide world-class service. *It is vital in professional services to retain the strongest possible service relationships.* Therefore, your training and development efforts with your team are an investment in your assets. When your staff members are motivated to share the same urgency toward client service, client expansion, and client value creation that you do, then you are liberated to stay in your peak zone. This also has the benefit of reducing office backbiting and jealousy over pay or perks as each established employee understands the payoffs of the broader goal and has a voice in compensation and performance issues.

What makes you a successful entrepreneur, your peak zone—or Kolbe—may not include the management of employees. Additionally, as the founder of the company, you had a dream and a passion that you should never expect to be found in employees whose peak zones include many of the administrative, personnel, and coordinating tasks you may despise. As a result, many of your employees are motivated in different ways than you. Additionally, they require different training and support to be successful at their jobs than you require.

Treating your employees as assets deepens their connection to your goals. Employees become models and informal coaches to other staff. Conversely, because the ownership mindset must reside in your culture, must be taught and modeled to others, and must be baked into the performance review and evaluation process, even talented employees who can't or won't share your client-centric model must be asked to leave.

"Whatever your cultural values, you must weed out those in the firm who cannot embrace those concepts," note Tibergien and Pomering. "No matter how big their economic contribution to the firm, people who set negative examples eventually sap the firm of its lifeblood. The long-term economic toll of bad apples is significant. Most firms that are successful in reinforcing behavior do so through a structured evaluation process through which peers evaluate peers, superiors evaluate subordinates, and subordinates evaluate superiors."[7] The authors note that the chairman of the consultancy Moss Adams, Bob Bunting, developed a statement of cultural values and incorporated it into all key processes, including "the staff's upstream appraisals of their supervisors. . . . Imagine the impact on a partner when he or she receives multiple staff assessments questioning the partner's demonstration of integrity and respect."[8]

The liberated CEO needs to give employees the time and mentoring to grow into the professionals you want them to be. Anyone who has taught in a classroom, patiently managed employees over a long period of time, or even parented will know this is not easy. Nor is it easy to build a great team of employees to think like an owner. How are family businesses able to eventually move the next generation into successful leadership of the organization? They treat the next generation as future owners, and mentor them all the way through the business—from the mailroom to the corner office. In effect, they are promoting from within the firm, too. Family members being groomed to eventually take over the business are many times given much more leeway to learn and make mistakes. While we understand the family reasons for taking such patience to mentor a family member, I propose that working with all employees in such a manner will create a much stronger company, from top to bottom.

If you approach your employees as if they are eventually your legacy within the firm, you will spend the time and resources to help them be as successful as they can. You will be committed to helping them over their own hurdles and finding their own peak zones.

Not every employee has the skills to eventually run your firm, nor does every child. However, unlike children, when you hire someone, you at least get to pick who you are starting with as a possible successor.

COMMUNICATING THE BIG PICTURE

You can and should implement every one of the actions we discuss to instill an ownership mindset. Because everyone on any job also has a myriad of responsibilities, interests, and family concerns (and, after all, they're not Quick Starts who began a business) as well as the pressure of their current tasks, it can be very difficult at one time or another for staffers to keep the big picture in mind of why the firm's success and values are so important. It's vital that you make the strategies in this chapter a regular topic of discussion and chat around the office. You can praise and reward employees when they show TLO chops, informally raise aspects of the strategies at staff meetings, and share good news about the company's successes and financial growth. Talk about how a particular management concern needs to be addressed and what you plan to do about it. Share how the media, experts, and competitors are talking about the firm and, when the talk is positive, how that reflects on the work of individual team members. One effective practice at staff meetings is to rotate presentations where each employee picks out a current challenge and seeks the coaching of his colleagues on fresh ideas for addressing it.

When appropriate, include different employees in the bigger picture decisions of the firm. Seek out their advice. Brainstorm with them. Let them know that you value their input. When you do something contrary to their thoughts, let them know why, or show them that your final decision was not what you were initially thinking and that their input was valuable—as I am sure that it truly was. As a Quick Start myself, I tend to make quick decisions. By slowing down and talking these through with employees, I am able to make a more informed decision. The more I am removed from the day-to-day operations, the more I need this input.

By soliciting the advice of employees, you are gaining their respect and trust, while at the same time helping them to TLO.

FIXING THE PROCESS BEFORE YOU BLAME THE PEOPLE

In a TLO culture, employees want to succeed on the company's terms. Employees work hard on the right things (in our case, customer relationships). Structured feedback means everyone is talking and taking accountability for decisions and performance. If your people are assets, you don't wear them down with criticism and blame, which every neuroscientist and psychologist knows keeps our brains in a threat state that diminishes creative, productive thinking. That's why at Navigoe, we build all our processes to serve people, not the other way around. If a decision or interaction does not succeed, we re-examine and test the process first, not the person. This represents another reason we install checklists and automated workflows: By focusing on the process when a mistake or breakdown occurs, we capture this knowledge and record it immediately. In this way, we practice continual improvement, both in terms of the employee who may have made a mistake and also ongoing office operations.

We have seen the importance of this perspective for some time in our careers. There is a new employee, with great references, and a good interview. Then someone complains about the numerous mistakes made by the new employee. That starts the vicious cycle of more mistakes, and more criticism. Soon there is office gossip . . . is this new employee going to make it? When this happened in our office, I stepped in.

The first thing I did was spend time with the experienced employee and her immediate supervisor to evaluate the mistakes that were being made. What became very clear was that we had done a very poor job of training the new employee. I immediately saw that without exception the issues being faced by our new employee corresponded with failures and gaps in our processes. Because this employee was our first new hire in some time, the rest of the team knew the appropriate steps but had failed to update the workflows, and no one had thought about it because they knew the particular requirements in question. Our meetings solved three problems very quickly.

1. We reassured a deeply worried employee who began operating at the high level we had expected.
2. I went to the coworker who had complained the most and assigned her to help with the training our new hire should have received from the beginning.
3. Most important, we hired a consultant (outsourced a task that does not directly touch our clients) to help us re-engage with the continuous improvement of our checklists and workflows.

This got all the team thinking more like an owner, forced us to improve our systems, and demonstrated the need for continual evaluation of systems.

This isn't just true of Navigoe or financial planners as an industry. Great managers know people aren't perfect but perfectible—that is, able to learn, develop new skills, grow as professionals, provided they are coached informally and formally. When there is a mistake or a missed opportunity, train yourself to ask the question, why? Then, follow the answers where they lead. In many cases, the answers are not due to negligence or egregious error, but a systemic glitch or unforeseen event. In thinking about employees as possible future owners of the company, you focus your energy on proper mentoring, rather than instilling fear of being fired. It allows everyone to realize that we are all in this together, and we all need to work together to continue to have *our* business grow and prosper.

Remember the true story about the invention of the checklist through the crashes of bomber prototypes? The key to perfecting the B-29 was found through analyzing the process, not blaming the test pilots. The aviation industry and the Air Force even commission exhaustive studies to identify what leads to human error in accidents, and how to engineer aircraft and change safety programs to adjust for common errors.[9]

"Success is not final, failure is not fatal: it is the courage to continue that counts," Winston Churchill remarked (and when Churchill and the Conservative Party were voted out of office after World War II he didn't blame a soul but went to work strengthening the party's platform and role in post–World War II British society where the overwhelming concern was rebuilding social and educational institutions). Leadership expert Marshall Goldsmith observed about the finger pointing that went on during the 2008 financial crash, that effective managers and professionals were those who would "help more, and judge less"[10] during a crisis. Managers who are quick to blame also suppress risk-taking and initiative as employees fear retribution and backlash from making mistakes. The legendary coach and leader John Wooden of UCLA was fond of quoting his Purdue coach Piggy Lambert who said, "The team that makes the most mistakes wins." A powerful example of how this perspective on leadership works can be found in the remarkable comeback of media-streaming and DVD-rental company Netflix— now one of the hottest stocks around and a hugely admired business.

In 2011, Netflix CEO Reed Hastings had the best analysis—that consumers would prefer streaming content with multiple devices rather than dealing with DVDs—but his management team misread that analysis to make a number of misguided calls. Netflix announced it would create a streaming-only service, separate out its DVD business, and charge customers who rented DVDs in those familiar red sleeves more than new streaming-only buyers. They in effect announced they were going to punish their most loyal and longest-held customers! More than 800,000 customers quit the service, and the Netflix team compounded the error by complaining about red ink and threatening to sell the company—in effect blaming their best customers once again. It didn't take long however for Hastings to accept responsibility, apologize to his customers, talk openly of his embarrassment, and begin a comeback by reanalyzing their customer base and content strategy. No one was ceremoniously fired and no other company or trend was blamed to appease the media or Wall Street. Netflix began surveying and talking to customers, and realized their loyal customer base was their most important asset. These customers would prove to be the leading adopters of streaming, and aficionados of the deep libraries of quirky movies, classic TV series, and hidden film gems available on the streaming platform. Netflix returned to its core value of keeping its customer base happy—all while compiling sophisticated analytics about what they spend and why they spend it on their platform.

With this edge Netflix began producing original content such as *House of Cards* and *The Killing* that excite and appeal to Netflix customer groups. As of 2013, their stock is rising steadily and customers are ecstatic. Wharton marketing professor Eric Bradlow noted of their revival, "The company hasn't missed a beat—besides that hiccup. . . . They have stayed with the vision and rolled with the times. The vision centers on valuing the customer by calculating their lifetime value to the company and making tangible decisions about how to find them."[11]

Of course, we have many examples of professionals making bad calls because of institutional, political, monetary, or career pressures, or because of significant personality flaws. There are times when you have the wrong people in a job, or the wrong relationship with an outside vendor or client. The real estate bubble of the 2000s occurred because of systemic problems—lack of appropriate regulation or legal guidance in making mortgages available—that attracted mortgage brokers and bankers who had a greed problem, or built their business around their greed problem and pressured employees to sell mortgages to folks whose finances made them bad risks. In a service or small business, there are times, of course, when you must let people go. It's critical that you go about this with sensitivity; for long-term employees, consider transition packages including severance benefits. Smaller firms drawing on regional and local client communities can be hurt by negative word of mouth from former, disgruntled employees.

With many smaller firms, your local reputation is extremely important to your success. Having a disgruntled ex-employee in the community can quickly erode all the good will you and your firm have established. By treating your employees equally, and doing everything in your power to help them grow and prosper, by being a fair mediator of strife when it occurs, you are instilling trust and respect in every relationship at work. If it becomes time to let an employee go, hopefully they also know deep down that they are just not the correct person for the firm, and that you have tried over and over to help them be successful.

If you reach that point, you will have a series of difficult conversations with that employee, from advising them of the issues you've noticed, to potentially giving them a warning, and eventually advising them of separation. Human beings never like rejection and you want to be prepared for these moments. Most of all, you need to give the situation the time it needs and respect the situation of the person losing their job. I'd recommend a number of resources to get ready for these situations, including the *New York Times* bestseller *Crucial Conversations: Tools for Talking When Stakes Are High*, by Kerry Patterson, Joseph Grenny, Ron Macmillan, and Al Switzler; *Perfect Phrases for Managers and Supervisors*, by Meryl Runion; and the chapter "The Art of Tough Love" in the bestselling classic *First, Break All the Rules*, by Marcus Buckingham and Curt Coffman.

Having a fair severance package is also part of treating the employee with respect. It shows that you appreciate the work and effort that they gave for the firm. It shows that you hold no ill feelings toward the person. It is just a decision that was necessary for the firm to continue to grow. In most cases, separations from the workplace are really about the wrong job for the person, not that there is anything fundamentally wrong with the person.

The way you work with employees who are struggling to fit into your organization, and the way in which you finally help them move on to other opportunities, is very telling and important to current employees and is key to leading by example. You are showing how much you value your employees, and how willing you are to help them be successful. You demonstrate that people can make mistakes while attempting to grow and become better. The message you are sending to current employees by treating a failing employee very fairly is much more valuable than the short-term costs associated with a proper termination.

LINKING COMPENSATION TO THE APPROPRIATE PERFORMANCE

Fair, generous compensation tied to performance is a major factor in running a liberated business that allows you to stay in control and have the life you want. The counterpoint to this is the legal profession that still operates on an hourly model. As a result, lawyers are compensated to do the research, every single time, to reinvent the wheel, with every contract they write. Is it any wonder that most clients have a love/hate relationship with their attorney?

Attorneys and accountants could be very successful with our model; but since they are still mainly compensated by the hour, there is a disincentive to adopt some of the efficiencies and productivity measures we discuss. If you run a business on an hourly fee model, your compensation structure will not support or motivate people to adopt the TLO mindset. Rather, employees are motivated to extend the time to complete a task or service, up to whatever point where integrity would be at stake. Even if a professional can deliver a good result in half the time of a competitor, they won't be motivated to deliver that value to the client. Hourly billing can become a major block to innovating systems to better leverage the resources of your business. Eventually, this will have the effect of limiting true profitability as it relates to all the different levels of employees within the company. Why? Because all the incentives are aligned with employees increasing their compensation by being able to charge more per hour, not by innovating ways to be more efficient and productive.

The business of a liberated CEO is focused on client satisfaction and service, and the results that deliver that satisfaction. Tracking and recording hours will be helpful for understanding and measuring tasks internally, but have no relevance to the client. We hold that performance-based compensation should apply to over 90 percent of your employees in a professional services firm. It needs to be simple and understandable to all, and it needs to be structured to truly motivate your team without being a hindrance. Employees must see true cause-and-effect outcomes on their pay as a result of overall business performance and the performance of individual clients with whom they work.

This book's strategies are a system because all the steps are connected and reinforce one another. Remember how we recommend outsourcing all non-client-facing work? That's about alignment of roles, outcomes, and strategy: We want team members who serve our clients or manage our clients' money, to have their financial incentives aligned with mine. Conversely, having performance-based pay for a bookkeeper isn't needed or even in alignment. We want a bookkeeper to maintain accounts to independent, legally and financially appropriate standards, not our firm's business blueprint.

The pay of client-facing staff and any personnel who deal with the revenue-generating side of your business should be tied to the true net profit of the entire company. You are building a team and company culture; compensation should be based on the teams' results and the individual's achievements that align with the company's goals. At Navigoe, for many of our employees, over half their annual compensation comes from a measurement other than pure salary. We have low base salaries with a high participation in different forms of incentive pay. None of this will work as it should, however, if you have the wrong incentives and if your compensation ends up confusing your crew. Most employees do not in the moment decide to deliver good or bad service based on their incentive pay. The benefits to them and your firm are about strengthening and developing a culture of service and performance. It is also about getting them to Think Like an Owner.

To liberate the potential of your team and get their oars pulling together, your incentive compensation plan should be built on three basic elements:

1. Individual achievements.
2. Team achievements.
3. Bonus achievements.

INCENTIVE COMPENSATION BASICS

To liberate the potential of your team and get their oars pulling together, your incentive compensation plan should be built on three basic elements:

1. A range of 10 to 40 percent of an employee's total compensation should be based on *individual achievements*. Each employee should have individual targets they can reach without competing or collaborating with other staff. The goals should be clearly stated, reasonable to obtain, and easily measureable.

(*continued*)

2. Team or firm achievements should comprise about 5 to 25 percent of a team member's compensation—a smaller share than individual achievements because, behaviorally, people will only tolerate so much of their pay being outside of their individual control. Imperative: close alignment with your strategic plan.

3. Bonus pay differs from other performance compensation in that it rewards above-and-beyond accomplishments often involving enterprise and risk. This amount should be no more than 10 percent of total compensation.

We recommend that a range of 10 to 40 percent of an employee's total compensation is based on *individual achievements* relating to service quality, productivity, compliance, and process improvements. (The range is so large since we are talking about employees at all levels within a company. Some may have fewer individual achievements but more team achievements.) Each employee should have individual performance targets they can reach without competing or collaborating with other staff. The performance goals should be *clearly stated, reasonable to obtain, and easily measurable*. For an accounting firm, these might contain the number of clients served per year, client evaluations, metrics on tax preparation mistakes or audits, and innovations in marketing the firm's thought leadership on tax preparation and financial management. In a financial advisory firm, a client–administrative specialist's individual targets could include client evaluations, quality of material, matrix around minimizing errors and implementing process, continued education and perfection of duties, or helpfulness as a team player.

In a communications and public relations consultancy, an account manager's targets might comprise new business referrals from the manager's client base, media list accuracy, client-satisfaction ratings, and innovative social media strategies. Particularly in small offices, there's a limit to how much direct competition you should foster among your managers and key staff. Each employee should have targets they can reach without limiting another employee's opportunities. Additionally, rewards around individual achievements do not have to be purely financial. Getting to leave early on a Friday because their work is completed can be as strong a motivator as anything.

Team or firm achievements should comprise about 5 to 25 percent of a team member's compensation—a smaller share than individual achievements because, behaviorally, people will only tolerate so much of their pay being outside of their individual control. Imperative: close alignment with your strategic plan. These incentives must help people feel good about the whole organization and its progress; they should not be aligned with trends over which the employee has no control, such as assets under management, which is affected by market trends. Metrics I recommend include profit margin, client retention, efficiency measures, client service evaluations, industry rankings, and awards where appropriate. Some of these can be ongoing, consistent measures, such as profit sharing. Others may be shorter term, such as the full implementation of a new CRM system. Remember, if you as the principal are recognized by the industry for an award, that metric reflects well on the entire organization and should be treated as such. It is essential that your performance goals reinforce your cultural and strategic plan.

Finally, bonus pay is also essential. Bonus pay differs from other performance compensation in rewarding enterprising, at-risk initiatives that fall outside core performance requirements. We recommend that this amount comprise no more than 10 percent of total compensation. For nonprincipals, this can consist of recruiting new clients, recommending a new cost-saving process, or generating positive publicity for the company. For principals, consider industry achievements, serving on high-profile boards, government appointments, or writing and publishing a business book.

This is a TLO compensation strategy. It can't exist in a vacuum if it is going to truly work. Also, it should not be designed in a vacuum. A poorly implemented strategy can be worse than no plan at all. There is no activity more important for a TLO culture than including employees in designing their own compensation package. If you are an executive of the firm and performing professional duties, and you are also an owner, you should be compensated as an employee and as an owner. As a CEO or senior executive, your base pay should be in the range that is appropriate for someone to take over your duties. The same is true for other members of your team, of course.

As we said earlier, as employees become settled into a job, they simply don't consider their incentive plans during their moment-by-moment workflow. Leaders must engage their team in management decisions and provide the training and support so they understand how their compensation works and how their firm operates. (I see this approach as more important to sustaining a TLO culture and way of working than what determines the highest bonus.) That's the topic of the final element of TLO.

PARTICIPATION, TRAINING, AND TRANSPARENCY

Pretty simple: If you want folks to think like owners, treat them that way. Compensation needs to be part of excellent management. As your firm grows, you will have more decisions to make because you'll have more people and more issues. As a liberated CEO you'll need the discipline and vision to engage your entire slate of owners in many management decisions. This ultimately keeps you in your peak zone. When you share the decision making, you spend less time selling a choice because you've discussed and worked through broad consensus.

You're also working to sustain the TLO culture by having business-owner conversations with your employees. You're talking about whether to hire a new employee becomes a team decision, for example. You're sharing how the cost of the new employee will come directly out of the profit pool, but that employee should be able to free up some time and as a result help to increase the profit over time. New computers, flex Fridays, client events: these all become decisions you discuss with the group. They will feel the pain when too many staff go on vacation at the same time, or if the company loses a client. As new clients are added they earn more, not just work more. When new employees are being interviewed, key personnel who will be working with the new hire participate. When your office lands a big contract or faces a series of tough deadlines, your ownership culture means folks will find it easier to stay late and work long hours when it is really needed.

If you've spent a few years taking pride in making all the management decisions, this transition will not be comfortable at first. Start slow: We recommend you start with bringing team members into the interview process with prospective hires. Every staff member will be interested in the potential new colleague, and since everyone goes through interviews, the experience is familiar.

Give your employees a copy of this book. Talk about the concepts and the steps with them. Let them understand that you want to implement all the steps in the book, including a re-evaluation of the compensation plan for employees. Discuss the steps together, and make a plan to implement them together. Assign chapters of the book to different employees to read closely and present to you and the rest of your staff. Implementation of the steps in the book can be a great initial matrix for bonuses and incentive compensation. It will be easier to execute many of the steps if your employees know the whole process, and can see the bigger picture. You will see the power of starting with the end in mind, for everyone in the firm.

You can't expect your team to magically meet all the expectations of TLO on their own. Humans are learners and highly adaptable, but they need coaching and the right content. "One of the most glaring gaps in the human capital capabilities of advisors is their lack of ability or interest in training, coaching, developing and mentoring others in their organization," note Tibergien and Pomering. They cite one case of a financial advisor/CEO who hired them to instill manager evaluations both up and down their firm's hierarchy, and train staff in using the instruments effectively. It took *three years* for the training and evaluations to really take hold and change the culture, resulting in better efficiency and profitability. At Navigoe, our training commitment includes continuing education, mentoring, positive feedback, and, where needed, constructive criticism.

Now where does all this advice lead in your journey from solo practitioner to liberated leader? Remember, early in the chapter we said that these TLO virtues include reinforcing loyalty, aligning with core strategy, fortifying your business's values, sustaining your succession plan, and encouraging continuous learning of key professional skills. Call it the TLO difference: your talent development strategy for keeping a loyal crew. Each aspect of our approach helps make these virtues sustainable, from treating your employees as valued assets, to communicating the ownership vision, to fixing the process before you blame the people, to performance-linked compensation, to radically expanded transparency and participation.

We should keep in mind the words of the scholar and management thinker Peter Drucker who, in one of his final articles, published in the 2002 *Harvard Business Review*, said "The attenuation of the relationship between people and the organizations they work for represents a grave danger to business." Businesses must think of their human assets, not as just employees, Drucker said, but as people who can bring a great deal of advantage to the organization. In fact, the last line of the article sums it up: "Employees may be our greatest liability, but people are our greatest opportunity."[12]

In the next chapter, we will offer more detailed guidance on the various financial ownership options and formulas that fit your particular business. And we'll show you how everything we've discussed to this point puts a business in the strongest position for sale and succession.

Even if you or your colleagues are not thinking about selling your company in the near future, running it and having the accounting, compensation, roles, and delivery of services set up so that it is ready to be sold at any moment is the culmination of all that we have talked about and the ultimate measure of liberation.

KEEP A LOYAL CREW AND THE TLO
SECRET KEYS TO THE CHAPTER

The success of the liberated CEO depends on developing a workplace culture where each member of your team is thinking like an owner. When done properly the TLO strategies outlined in this chapter will help change your organization from a personal-service firm to a true business, with a long-term expectation of longevity beyond its founder. Developing a TLO mindset requires following these, among other, steps:

- View employees as assets, like clients, not liabilities like computer equipment. Family businesses offer useful lessons in the value of mentoring, training, and developing talent—such as giving people leeway to make mistakes and learn, which pays off in the longer run with a stronger company from top to bottom.
- Communicate the big picture. Liberated CEOs must not only communicate openly about day-to-day business and client concerns, but share aggressively about the financial and operation realities of a business and what it must do to be profitable and create wealth.

- Fix the process before you blame the people. Great managers know that people aren't perfect but perfectible.
- Link compensation to the appropriate performance. This model isn't enough on its own to build a TLO culture, but it is the most transformative of a culture in the context of an entire strategy.
- Manage culture through participation, training, and transparency. If you want people to think like owners, treat them that way.

NOTES

1. Josh Patrick, "The Real Meaning of Corporate Culture," *You're the Boss* (blog), *New York Times*, May 21, 2013, http://boss.blogs.nytimes.com/2013/05/21/the-real-meaning-of-corporate-culture/?_r=0.
2. Edward Coates, "Profit Sharing Today, Plans and Provisions," *Monthly Labor Review*, April 1991, and Schaffner Van Horn, "Profit Sharing," in *Work in America: An Encyclopedia of History, Policy and Society* (Santa Barbara, CA: ABC-CLIO, 2003).
3. Ibid.
4. Joseph Blasi and Douglas Kruse, "Employee Stock Ownership," in *Work in America: An Encyclopedia of History, Policy and Society*, Schaffner Van Horn (Santa Barbara, CA: ABC-CLIO, 2003).
5. Mark Tibergien and Rebecca Pomering, *Practice Made (More) Perfect*, (Hoboken, NJ: John Wiley & Sons, 2011).
6. Ibid.
7. Ibid.
8. Ibid.
9. Scott Shappell and Doug Wiegmann, "HFACS Analysis of Civilian and Military Aviation Accidents," ISASI, 2004, http://asasi.org/papers/2004/Shappell%20et%20al_HFACS_ISASI04.pdf.
10. Marshall Goldsmith, "7 Steps to Stop Fingerpointing in a Crisis," *Harvard Business Review Blog Network*, October 1, 2008, http://blogs.hbr.org/goldsmith/2008/10/7_steps_to_stop_finger_pointin.html.
11. Knowledge at Wharton, "On Wall Street, Netflix Is a Comeback Kid—But Can It Stay on Top?," June 5, 2013, http://knowledge.wharton.upenn.edu/article.cfm?articleid=3275.
12. Carl Van Horn, *Working Scared or Not at All* (Lanham, MD: Rowman & Littlefield, 2013).

CHAPTER 8

MADE TO SELL: CHANGING THE WATCH

So far, you've learned seven strategies that empower you to climb to your ultimate goal—to become a liberated CEO. We've shown how your success depends on staying in your peak zone and out of the dead zone, where your business ascent can paradoxically trap you in the crosswinds of chaotic growth. We've shown you how our methods provide the leverage that allows your firm to break through the service business ceiling. As we've learned, owners and principals can't achieve these goals alone; it's also about your crew and their long-term success. One of the great satisfactions of leading a service business is that you have the liberty and capability to develop employees over a long period of time and benefit from their professional growth. While the title of our book speaks to leaders, our strategies help every committed professional stay in their peak zone.

Remember, you can deploy our ideas at different times and in the sequence that fits your situation. You may not need all of the steps if your business is newer or remains smaller than five people. To reach a particular goal, you may need to lean on one or two steps more than others. Over the cycle of a successful business, however, you are quite likely to need all of the steps. And for you and your team, selling the business isn't the final box to be checked, but an everyday reminder of what it takes to be a liberated CEO. In fact, much of our book has been about getting to the point where the founder and CEO is irrelevant to the day-to-day operations of the company, because your core employees have realized their full potential as professionals. This may be the point where your firm is at its highest value.

At any one time, understanding how all the steps interact can mean the difference between success and failure. As my family and I return to the United States after our trip sailing the high seas, Navigoe is primed and prepared for a major period of growth—an opportunity that would have been impossible without the amazing success of these approaches. We're not selling our business, but when that day comes, we know we'll be prepared for that transition in ownership and what it means. What will your business be worth when it is sold and what can be done to ensure it is sold at the maximum price? This question is the culmination of everything you and I have been and are working for. While the point of our book is not to sell your business before the right time, everything we advise is offered to lead to the highest value at whatever time your business is ultimately sold. Most of all, don't procrastinate or assume you'll know what to do years in the future. In a white paper developed by Echelon Partners, consultants to the wealth and investment management industries, the authors summarized the way many CEOs and partners view continuity and succession planning: "Continuity planning, likes its close relative, succession planning, is an endeavor that many wealth managers know they have to address at some point but often never get around to designing, drawing up, and implementing. As a result, they unwittingly put their firms and beneficiaries at risk by neglecting to prepare their practices for the unthinkable."[1]

Nailing your business's exit strategy is a major test for the liberated CEO; meeting the challenge ensures that the wealth you create is not dissipated by making the sale to the wrong buyer or at the wrong time or for the wrong reasons. In the first part of this chapter, we build on what we learned about the TLO mindset. We'll demonstrate that keeping a loyal crew means allowing key employees to own shares in your business and participate in the future value of the business they help create. In the second part, we guide you through the key principles for sustaining and building business value so it appeals to potential buyers. We discuss how to sustain profitability, how to think about the business for selling, and the important processes you'll need to master along the way.

We address a common question among executives and CEOs: Will the clients remain with the firm under new ownership after the owners depart (most often the seller stays on for a transitional period) and how can that be encouraged? To the extent the profit of the company is less reliant upon any individual(s), the higher the multiple available for the firm. The simplest path to this outcome is through building the capacity of the firm's internal team. Because the more clients can identify with the entire firm as a service brand, rather than a single individual, the more confidence they will have in a transition of ownership.

As we discussed in Chapter 7, building a TLO culture will result in a range of positive behaviors. The next level of engagement for your team is asking who is ready for a long-term commitment. What happens when you make key employees actual owners of your business? If we're recruiting long-term owners from our loyal crew, what type of employee should become an eventual partner?

IF YOU OWN IT, YOU DON'T BREAK IT

Remember the phrase coined by columnist Thomas Friedman and famously quoted by General Colin Powell, "the Pottery Barn rule of foreign policy"—if you break it, you own it (if the President of the United States initiates a military action, he or she will be held responsible for everything that takes place afterwards). Let's reverse that in thinking about the effects of bringing your crew into ownership positions with your firm—if they own it, they don't want to break it. Selling ownership to the next generation helps maintain loyalty, and gets people to think as owners, and ultimately can allow for a smooth succession and sale if there is an internal buyer group. When key employees participate in share or stock ownership, they not only think like owners but they begin to act like them. Folks are more willing to work the late nights when required. They begin to see how every decision impacts the P&L, from benefit costs to client management to the cost of office space.

Remember, when sharing ownership with employees, it is *not* a gift. They have to buy into the company. Equity and profit sharing should always be linked to performance and behavior, as with all other forms of compensation. Technically, there are six types of compensation for an owner in a business:

1. Base pay.
2. Performance-linked incentives that we discussed in the previous chapter.
3. Employee-based profit sharing as discussed in the previous chapter
4. Perquisites and health benefits.
5. Retirement plan matching and/or contributions.
6. Owners' compensation, which is based on firm profit and dividends.[2]

We refer you to the abundance of resources available to further research health and retirement plans and benefits; we're focusing on 1, 2, 3, and 6 as particularly strategic for the professional services firm.

Performance-linked compensation and broader company-wide profit sharing is essential but it doesn't mean you have to offer ownership to everyone. The type and number of employees to whom you offer ownership depend on your situation and type of workforce. Employee owners will need a higher level of commitment, caring, and continuity with the firm.

Whom should you welcome into an ownership plan, and why? We regard all professional-level employees (or those on a professional track through certification or training) as potential owners. For financial services, start qualifying with the paraplanning position and consider everyone above that position. With an accounting firm, the first qualifying position could be certified public accountants (CPAs) or enrolled accountants (EAs) and above. At law firms, paralegals may start the qualifying level.

Consider employees who have demonstrated success by adding value to the firm above and beyond performing their core duties, and who are capable of taking a long-term view of the company. Since there are other types of compensation to reward valued performers, you want to think about focusing on people who could be future partners of the firm. As you start to share ownership in a small firm with top performers, they are, in a way, making partner. That is one way to think of it. If you decide to sell the firm internally or to an outside buyer, building loyalty with key employees is critical.

For the sake of simplicity in discussing approaches to equity compensation, we are going to focus on the limited liability company (LLC). While much of what we talk about can be accomplished with corporations too, we are assuming that the LLC is the most common form of small business and will restrict our examples to that type of entity. None of this discussion is intended as legal advice.

While an LLC is limited to 100 shareholders, for most small businesses that is more than enough slots for moving key employees to owners. Another advantage of the LLC structure is that it offers leadership a great deal of flexibility in how ownership and management roles are aligned. This flexibility in effect allows the owner/founder to sell the majority of the company to employees while still maintaining full control of the company. While we are not suggesting this as a strategy, it is important to keep in mind when one looks at ways to provide ownership to key employees. So with an LLC, you can give employees ownership without giving them any control.

A vehicle for providing ownership to employees is the use of an employee stock purchase plan (ESPP). The ESPP is growing in popularity and has many advantages. These types of plans are fairly common with large, publicly traded companies. While some employees resist taking advantage of them, those who do express satisfaction with the benefit. As financial advisors, we often see clients who have a large percentage of their wealth tied up in their company's stock. It can be difficult to persuade clients to sell that stock when it is time to do so, because they have many positive emotional ties as employees of the firm.

Establishing a way to give ownership to employees of a small, privately held firm is more difficult. However, the long-term loyalty established from key employees is well worth the process. One of the most difficult tasks will be actually putting a fair price on the value of the equity of the firm.

By establishing a constant way to value shares, a faitly small company can establish an ESPP or a structure that acts similarly. This allows the owners to start selling shares at a very favorable tax situation and diversify their own asset base. With this type of plan, you can offer vesting periods as well as forced buyback periods. It may take 5 or even 10 years of employment for prospective owners to be eligible to purchase shares, and then if they leave for any reason, they could be forced to sell the shares. This way, a key employee can still benefit from helping to grow and develop a privately held company without having to stay around for some possible, future buyout. Part of this is helping key employees feel good about the best long-term advantages for the company, and be willing to spend the added time to build the firm. The great aspect with an LLC is that you get to create the rules. And they need to be fair, easy to understand, and transparent. (See the sidebar on page 125 for more on ESPPs and other major equity compensation plans.)

As we say to our clients all the time, it is important that you seek the services of a qualified attorney. As mentioned earlier, it is way beyond the scope of this book, or my expertise, to provide legal advice. Additionally, there are many different ways to set up the sharing of ownership with employees, such that the subject alone could fill a couple of books. The purpose of sharing these ideas here is to open up the concepts of shared ownership now, early in the life cycle of the company, as a strategy to build a highly motivated and loyal team. After all, the best way to get employees to think like owners is to have them be owners.

One of the benefits of an internal sale is that this opportunity becomes a motivation to employee owners who are not rainmakers or senior partners but nonetheless valued members of the workforce. In professional services firms, there's always a great deal of attention focused on the rainmakers who bring in the most business. But the whole question of profit is not only about revenue, but costs, management, and operations. You need other players who are incentivized to think through the pros and cons of hiring a chief operations officer or compliance officer, for example, knowing that the costs of the hire will impact profit and must therefore allow the rainmakers of the firm to increase client revenue substantially. These kinds of decisions play out over three-to-five year time frames, and require that many members of your team work together for rewards that are not immediately achieved.

PLAYING YOUR OPTIONS

With thanks to the superb book, *Practice Made (More) Perfect*, by Tibergien and Pomering (John Wiley & Sons, 2011), here is a crib sheet of equity-plan options:

Employee Stock Purchase Plan (ESPPs): Employees are offered membership in a plan to buy shares of the company at a discount to fair market value or at book value. The firm can set forced buyback periods, and impose a service period before the shares are sold. Gains on the shares after purchase are subject to capital gains tax, while discounts are taxed as income. This is a plain vanilla, broad-based offering that can be seen as less exclusive than other approaches.

Nonqualified Stock Options (NQSOs): Employees are given the option to buy shares of the firm's stock in the future at fair market value when the option was granted. Individuals can exercise the option by paying for the shares in cash or stock; then, to cash out, the employee must find a buyer for the shares, a significant disadvantage in a private firm. This approach provides TLO incentives, but does not yield the right to participate in ownership decisions. Typically these grants require vesting or waiting periods. Employees are taxed on the difference between the strike price and the fair market value of the stock (notice that tax is owed even if the stock is not sold). The company can take a deduction equal to the income the employee earns.

Incentive Stock Option Plans (ISOs): These differ from NQSQs in that they carry tax advantages for employees. The ISOs can only be offered to employees, the strike and exercise price must be the same, the ISO plan must be board approved, and the options must be held for at least a year to benefit from tax protections. The employee's shares are not taxed as income when they are granted and exercised, but depending on the spread between fair market value and strike price, some employees' gains could trigger the alternative minimum tax.

Phantom Stock: Fictional units of stock that the employee can exercise without coming up with the cash or stock to purchase. Units are granted with an established payment date. The firm must make

(continued)

> the payment in cash when the "stock" is cashed out, which becomes taxable income to the employee and a deduction for the firm.
> **Stock Appreciation Rights (SARs):** Similar to phantom stocks, but employees are given a longer period of time in which to exercise the option, rather than a date certain.
> **Restricted Stock:** Blocks of shares granted to employees that are not transferable, do not accrue dividends, and are forfeitable until the employee reaches a defined period of service, such as five years. Restricted stock retains its values for employees even if the shares do not appreciate (which makes stock options, SARs, and phantom stock worthless). The employee becomes a shareholder directly with voting and other rights. Employee can choose to be taxed at the time of the award or when the period of required job tenure is achieved.

PROFITS AND THE 60–20–20 FORMULA

A key theme of this chapter is that the true value of any company is profit. That is what your buyer wants to acquire. Liberated CEOs welcome employees who think like sellers and believe that by sharing the profit pie, they will grow the pie. But each business will need to decide on the formula for contributions to the ownership incentive plan. It is unreasonable to assume that your employees would forego income today to buy into a privately held company, for some possible, future payoff down the road. Their percentage ownership needs to include regular payouts from profits, and the shares they own should be fairly valued and that value updated regularly, so they are guaranteed their shares reflect the growth of the company if it occurs.

The most common measure of profits is called EBITA, an acronym that refers to a company's earnings before the deduction of interest, tax, and amortization expenses. I like to think of it a little differently, and more simply, too. For most small business owners, especially when starting out, our salary or compensation was simply whatever was left. For many of us in our earlier business years, that was a negative number. As we grew our firms, and became more successful, we actually started to pay ourselves on a regular basis, but much of our income was still what was left over. As a result, that is how we as owners tend to think about our revenue from our firms.

To become a liberated CEO, and start to bring in ownership with key employees, the whatever-is-left concept needs to be changed. Now this formula is not what the owner earns, but the actual, true profits of the company. To understand this properly, you need to do an exercise: Hire a replacement for yourself in the open market. If you were to stop working in the company, what would it cost to hire someone to replace you: salary, incentive pay, profit sharing, and so forth? Than that should become your pay. It's important to look externally to the market for an unbiased view of your value. As Warren Buffett once said, "Price is what you pay. Value is what you get."

Now, whatever is left is the profit of the company, and could be considered dividends and paid out to the owners of the company. (Not a true dividend in the sense of a publicly traded company, but I use the term as a differentiator. I am saying a dividend is paid to the owners of the company, for nothing more than being an owner of the company.)

For many of you, this will be much harder than it sounds. As we discussed in Chapter 7, setting up proper compensation can be complicated. I suggest using an outside consultant to help establish the firm's compensation plan. Then you can view the plan as a key employee and as an owner. This will help you to think about the compensation like your fellow employees do, and hopefully think about pay the same way they will.

For the top service firms, true dividend profits should be around the 20 to 30 percent of gross revenue. Our favored formula, if you're consistently profitable, is the 60-20-20 strategy. Under this formula, 60 percent of profit goes to owners based on ownership (the dividend), 20 percent is split among owners for predetermined ownership activities and their contribution to the firm, and 20 percent is shared with employees for their team-based incentive plans. In this example, employees may or may not include employee-owners who could also have additional stock options or the like.

Each firm can research and apply a mix of incentives for employee compensation and owner compensation. Your underlying philosophy is to consistently link compensation to performance for core employees across a spectrum of regular pay, bonuses, and profit sharing. For those employees who decided to buy into the company, they would also receive dividend payments as a percentage of their ownership. This dividend amount could be used as a major contributor to the ongoing valuation of the company.

By basing your ownership plan on the most critical factor for the financial health and sale of your firm—consistent profitability—and by having a large portion of that pure profit shared among the owners, you create a climate and culture where employees want to buy into ownership and perhaps buy the firm someday. The mindset among owners will be much more long-term than what you may find with other employees who are most concerned with their bonus or incentive compensation on a year-to-year basis.

Since this pure profit is the single largest factor of valuing a company for sale, we can deduce that profit is a key annual benchmark for determining the price of the company. Profitability and the value of your firm rise and fall together, so it is critical to understand and get key employees thinking about the factors that improve profit and valuation. That's the focus of our next section.

THE PILLARS OF VALUATION

Creating long-term incentives and ownership for key employees has many positive effects in cultivating a culture where employees think like owners and sellers and contribute to a firm's growth. In many ways, whatever makes a business more valuable to a buyer, means more value to you, the liberated CEO. What makes sense for the liberated CEO makes sense for the seller. If you're a captive of your business problems, it's unlikely your profits are percolating.

This discussion isn't about showing you exactly how to sell your company and when; those considerations are complex and driven by your circumstances and timing. It's about how you ensure your business increases in value and maintains its transferability to an internal or external owner.

What are our principles for maintaining and increasing the valuation of your firm?[3] First, know the life expectancy of your client base. Do you have a mix of younger and older clients? Can you show that you have a focused effort to market to clearly defined niches of potential clients? Don't market to every potential client in your region; develop an identity with a particular niche of client. Think deep and narrow. One successful accountant we know built most of his business with freelancers and independent creative professionals; the firm's reputation with this community results in a steady stream of new client referrals, a handsome asset for a prospective owner.

If your client base is older, the business implications are obvious. If that is the case, develop good relationships with the families of these clients, and you will likely increase the retention of your clients' children and grandchildren within the business. Second, maintain lean processes that allow for world-class customer service, including state-of-the-art technology and software that will be of great value to a new ownership team just as it is to you.[4]

Third, consistently put the client's interest ahead of your own. Do what is right and fair for the client. That can affect cash flow and profit in the near term, but will pay off in the long run. When I think back to the biggest trading error I ever made—I mistakenly executed a buy instead of a sell order—I knew technically we were not liable but I covered the difference through a personal check to the client who has remained with us ever since (more than 10 years).

Fourth, keeping a loyal crew is not only smart in the short run, it also encourages staff members to stay with the firm after the sale and provide familiar and trusted contacts for the client base.

Fifth, never forget about growth. According to Dan Seivert, CEO and managing partner at Echelon Partners, growth increases value because owners want to see growing revenue in the future, particularly because some older legacy clients may leave during the transition. If a firm has stagnated, "go back to the original business model to generate growth and add value. You are not going to get the premium for a firm that has stopped growing that you will get for one that is still growing."[5]

Sixth, maintain those open, ongoing communications with clients and customers so your team knows how your client base will respond to the sale or merger. This isn't an issue to address in the year before you sell; this is part of how the liberated CEO consistently manages her firm. You need to have a grasp of how clients view top partners and staff in the eventuality of an internal sale to a group within your firm. You also need to keep a lean, energetic, and disciplined mindset as a sale approaches—be careful of staff complacency, sloppy and excessive spending, or dropping your commitment to world-class service. Doing everything you can to train your team and develop your firm to be successful without you is the overriding factor. (You need to consider that many internal sales to senior employees will mean they will find it harder to raise the cash for the transfer of ownership and thus require financing. If you have an internal group that you see as a tremendous asset if they buy the firm, encourage them to get advice on securing capital and scenario planning.)

Finally, evaluate your profits and other metrics regularly, so that your team is building its mindset of thinking like a seller. According to CPA, consultant, and author John Ezell, your team should be tracking questions such as, "Is your market growing or declining? Are competitors looking to expand into your area? Are qualified local buyers interested in your practice?" And Ezell emphasizes that, "services, staff, clients, revenue, expenses, cash flow, profitability, fee mix, sale timing, and the demand for that type of practice and its geographic location will determine the firm's value to a buyer. The practice's cash flow, growth and stability—that is, its moneymaking capacity—will matter most."[6] Ezell confirms our point that "profitable practices usually generate higher selling prices and sell quickly."[7]

David Mahmood, founder and chairman of Allegiance Capital—a global investment banker who has sold eight of his own businesses—also emphasizes the critical factors of showing growth in sales and earnings, possessing a strong backlog of business, retaining an established management team, and having a good case to make about the market for your services, all backed by a long-term transition plan and understanding of the sale process.[8]

You may also want to hire an outside consultant or appraiser to assist in valuation. We all have an emotional attachment to the company we built . . . but we can't sell that attachment, so it is imperative to rely on a rational evaluation. When you are ready to begin the sales process, which includes selling some ownership to key employees, review the backgrounds of appraisers and get references. Also use sales of similar practices to yours to establish benchmark data. "Such data for private businesses aren't always easy to come by," notes the *Wall Street Journal*, "but some sites, such as BVMarketData.com, offer subscriptions to databases with business sales data."[9] However, it is critical to look at the terms of any sale, and understand what went into the valuation. It is very easy to get caught up in the industry shorthand, such as "three times gross revenue," which is seldom the true story behind any sale. If you are going to rely on shorthand, think of profits both present and future.

Ownership change will reveal the extent to which you've liberated your firm from the boutique mindset, and evolved as a true service brand business with the maturity, values, and service culture that will continue without the original founder-partners. Consider how admired and successful organizations have instilled a mindset for achievement and teamwork throughout their culture.

While the jury is still out as to whether Apple will produce as many world-changing innovations and sustain investor confidence without Steve Jobs, Apple's ability to, for the most part, sustain market share, brand loyalty, and consumer confidence speaks to how much Jobs did to instill the company with the practices and values that made it great. (And remember, Apple had to continue this process when Jobs became ill and left the company on sabbatical.)

Or reflect on the two most storied franchises in the NBA: the Boston Celtics and Los Angeles Lakers. Between the two of them, they have appeared in three-quarters of all the NBA finals and have won half. While their team executives build their teams for now, they also think toward the future, when the current players are long retired. It is a culture within the organizations that cause them to be dynasties. You can have Michael Jordan and be a dominant team for a decade. But you need an organizational mind-set that is very different to be a dynasty. It is no accident that the Lakers and Celtics are the two most valuable basketball franchises. The owner of the Lakers, Jerry Buss, recently passed away and his kids have taken over. While time will tell, I am willing to bet that the organization will continue to be a dominant organization going into the future.

The exit period for owners doesn't have to be a declining level of engagement ending up in a raid on the firm's coffers to pay for retirement. Owners can sell their firm at peak value, often to an internal team that worked with you for years to turn your small boutique shop into a thriving business. You'll need to know about valuation, compensation, and client expectations—and above all avoid procrastination!

**MADE TO SELL: CHANGING THE WATCH
KEYS TO THE CHAPTER**

Being prepared for transition in ownership and all it requires is the culmination of this book and everything you work for. While the point of our book is not to sell your business before the right time, everything we advise is offered to lead to the highest value at whatever time your business is ultimately sold. Nailing the exit strategy is a major test for the liberated CEO. We address a number of considerations. First, by keeping a loyal crew and selling ownership shares in your business, you enhance the prospects of a smooth succession and sale to an internal buyer group. We recommend considering the use of an employee stock purchase plan (ESPP) as a vehicle for providing ownership to employees. The ESPP is growing in popularity and has many advantages. Other equity plan options may make sense. We offer a formula for revenue sharing and distribution that places a strong emphasis on profits.

Whatever makes your firm more valuable to a buyer, makes more value for you, the liberated CEO—and your team. The following are among our principles for maintaining and increasing the valuation of your firm:

- Develop an identity with a particular niche of client; don't market to every type of client in your region.
- Maintain lean processes that allow for world-class customer service, including state-of-the-art technology and software.
- Consistently put the client's interests ahead of your own—it will pay off in the long run.
- Never forget about growth.
- Maintain open, ongoing communications with clients so your team knows how your client base will respond to the sale or merger.
- Evaluate your profits and other metrics regularly.

NOTES

1. Daniel Seivert, Aaron Jackman, Tyler Resh, and Eric Monroe, *How-to Guide on Continuity Planning* (Manhattan Beach, CA: Echelon Partners, 2009).
2. Mark Tibergien and Rebecca Pomering, *Practice Made (More) Perfect* (Hoboken, NJ: John Wiley & Sons, 2011).

3. Karen Demasters, "Advisory Firm Valuations Hinge on Many Factors," *Financial Advisor,* June 14, 2012.

4. Ibid.

5. Ibid.

6. John Ezell, "Build, Buy, (or Sell)?" *Journal of Accountancy*, April 2007, www .journalofaccountancy.com/Issues/2007/Apr/BuildBuyOrSell.htm.

7. Ibid.

8. David Mahmood, "6 Questions to Ask Before Selling Your Business," *Inc./* Inc.com, August 22, 2013, www.inc.com/david-mahmood/six-questions-to-ask-before-selling-your-business.html.

9. "How to Sell a Professional Practice," *Wall Street Journal*, http:// guides.wsj.com/small-business/buying-and-selling-a-business/ how-to-sell-a-professional-practice.

CHAPTER 9

BECOME AN EXPERT IN YOUR FIELD

My book and program are about empowering you with techniques and strategies that unleash your full potential as a business owner, value creator, and industry leader. But our system isn't about freeing up your time solely so you can get stale slogging through an ill-advised early semi-retirement, where you might spend more time at the mall, on the golf course, at the diner, or cradling your remote in front of your high-definition television. As you become more of a liberated CEO, you will encounter the responsibility of how to use the new time and freedom you enjoy.

In this chapter, I discuss why raising your profile as an expert, teacher, and/or thought leader is an amazingly productive benefit to living and leading as a liberated CEO. Building your brand as an expert or thought leader is not a hard science; however these elements are common to becoming an influencer in your field:

- Substantial credentials and experience in your profession with strong peer respect.
- A strong point of view on a business problem or problems.
- Demonstrated audience for that point of view and expertise.
- The resources and time to build a following or secure a teaching post or market a book.

- The willingness to create high quality content in terms of papers, speeches, books, or online articles.
- The savvy to position your content with a strong elevator pitch.

By studying, testing, and refining your core proficiencies in articles, speeches, association leadership, classroom teaching, or book publishing, you will reap many benefits for yourself, your family, network, and community. You will meet new potential collaborators and employees, help out your profession, give back to your industry, and avoid the risks of complacency. This last point is particularly relevant.

As your business moves through the maturity stage, a leading cause of decline is lack of innovation or keeping current with the competition. We all know the saying, "You can't teach an old dog new tricks." The self-satisfaction of successful business owners at the mature stage of their business cycle can be a curse. To maintain your operation at peak efficiency, you must continue to learn and improve your organization and instill that commitment in others.

We have all met experienced business owners and leaders who have built thriving enterprises, but stopped engaging with their industry. You know how it is when a peer tends to glaze over as a group of leaders are talking about the latest operational software or industry article. Most professions have continuing education requirements. If you're a lawyer, you have professional development requirements that ensure you don't get rusty. Doctors tend to have to keep up with research and pharmaceutical developments in their specialty. Nonetheless, complacency tends to seep in with success and dull your edge. Newton's laws of motion apply to human motivation—a body at rest tends to stay at rest and a body in motion tends to stay in motion.

As with each step in our program, becoming an expert in your field also helps you deliver on the promises you made to your clients during your career. By testing yourself in the arena of thought leadership, you force yourself to be challenged by high-performing peers and feed effective practices back into your firm. Naturally, by expanding your network and visibility, you attract new client opportunities.

For some of you, you will arrive at this step at a later stage in the evolution of the liberated CEO. You need to be confident in your expertise and in the operational efficiency of your business, division, or unit. You need the resources to encourage key players on your team to develop their expertise and visibility. I believe in training and professional development as a matter of course, and conferences are essential in this regard. Global organizations such as the American Society for Training and Development and the American Management Association train millions of people every year.

Events and conferences are particularly strategic for developing your brand as an expert and industry leader. It's not just about attending events; it's about how you approach them, in order to get the value you seek and to feel good about your participation. Naturally, you want to garner new competitive intelligence, and take steps to becoming a presenter or panelist. You may not be the most extroverted leader, but every one of us can draw on conference strategies to garner business ideas, more industry contacts, and leads for promoting your firm and your own expertise. Here are eight tips for making the most of these opportunities:

1. **Focus on professional associations.** Every business has professional associations where peers share practices, lessons, and fellowship. If it suits you, strive to be a leader in the organization at the local and then regional and national levels.

2. **Articulate your goals for the event first.** As leadership guru Don Pepper wrote, "Before even deciding to invest time and money in attending a conference, however, be clear on your goals. Do you want to consolidate existing relationships or meet new people? Do you want to acquire 'how to' expertise or to gather industry insights and intelligence? From a personal standpoint, are you trying to grow your 'personal brand' or make connections with others?"[1] In this chapter, we're singling out the importance of building your brand.

3. **Prepare for the conference and identify key players you want to meet.** Devote an hour or two over your morning coffee or tea a few days ahead to read the program, speaker, and attendee list. Decide on a few (five or less) significant leaders or experts with whom you wish to connect. Note the names of event organizers and leaders so you'll know to introduce yourself if you meet.

4. **If you come with a work colleague or friend, split up and conquer new relationships.** Sure, it's fine to deepen

collegial friendships at dinner or a reception, but the security blanket of a friend will hold you (and your colleague) back from your brand-building agenda. Make plans to see friends after the main events are concluded.

5. **Attend panels that offer new insights for your business, where your top competitors or peers are presenting, or focus on topics suitable for what you'd like to present.** Choose panel or breakout sessions carefully. Avoid the topics you already know well or that are outside your peak zone. I find it particularly strategic to look for events where my competitors are presenting, so I can learn what they're up to that I might be missing. If you're working to land a panel appearance or speaking slot in the years ahead, look for panels that are close to those you'd be suited for—and be prepared to introduce yourself to the organizers, and leave an introductory package with them if the timing feels right. At the minimum, get business cards and follow up after the conference.

6. **Don't take tech and software exhibitors for granted.** As we discussed in Chapters 4 and 5, leading-edge software can be an enormous competitive advantage. If your industry has tech or software vendors on the floor in areas such as finance, operations, human resources, new tax prep software, payroll, what have you, don't assume "it's just tech." Every industry can point to the small tech booth that was ignored one year and eventually became a disruptive force.

7. **Be generous—give and you'll get.** In meetings or discussions with competitors or leaders of bigger practices you want to emulate, be prepared with insights from your own successes and practices. Of course, reveal nothing truly proprietary or confidential, but every business has some successes you can share and explain. This will lubricate your peer discussions and lead to more in-depth conversations.

8. **If you use Twitter and Facebook, spread good news.** Tweet out or post accolades to good panels or meetings. People deeply appreciate this type of affirmation.

9. **Follow up with calls and/or personal notes.** If you plan to seek a panel or speaking post, share your accomplishments or key publications with the organizers and set up a phone

call. Drop a note to every new contact you met with and ask if there is a need for a follow-up chat (unless the meeting was truly unproductive).

THE REWARDS OF THOUGHT LEADERSHIP

As a liberated CEO who has mastered many of the steps discussed in this book, you may arrive at this step with more time to devote to teaching, speaking, writing, and expressing your expertise (and consider hiring a coach to help you with speaking or media training). Ultimately, this new direction could lead to a full-time career when you're ready to sell, resign, or step back from your business. Teaching is a valuable option that can complement your other activities. Whether you are primarily a franchise owner, store manager, operations whiz, finance expert, manufacturing leader, sales manager, accountant—colleges and universities are often looking for part-time or adjunct professors in their business and finance offerings. Start to teach. One of the best ways to truly master your craft, and more important, excel in expressing your unique benefit to your prospects and clients, is to teach.

This is all personally rewarding; it is also about giving back and sharing your knowledge and experience with younger professionals and various communities with which you are associated. I'm looking forward in the years ahead to working with the financial planning industry, as well as higher education and graduate business schools, to address the lack of a career path for the financial planning and advising world. Graduate business degrees offer specializations in finance and banking, but more schools need to offer course concentrations in the distinctive skills and knowledge required for financial planning and advising. Mine is a growing industry with good jobs often in smaller, more flexible, and family-friendly firms. Students and young professionals with finance skills need to be educated during their college and graduate years about the range of job opportunities available.

The Financial Planning Association (FPA) and other groups (working with the public sector and universities) need to conceive, study, and promote career paths as is done with investment banking or commodities trading. According to a 2009 poll by the FPA, 88 percent of financial planners and advisors say they worked in a different profession first. Many top graduates with finance and business interests don't have top-of-mind awareness of the financial planning and advising industry. This poses a major challenge for CEOs of developing practices everywhere in our field.

Where do your passions lie in improving your own profession, at a local, regional, or national level? You want to examine your own strengths and capabilities, as well as your visibility on various issues affecting your profession, as you consider what direction to take. Reach out to peers and friends and chat with them about how they view your particular strengths. You could devise a concise survey (you can use one of the online survey tools available such as Survey Monkey) that you offer to associates and friends. Here, you design no more than 10 questions that ask them to rate you and your firm on particular strengths and expertise; this can provide an external perspective on where your track record and business personality resonate with others. This is another version of the technique we mentioned in Chapter 2 about testing out big ideas with your close network. You'll further develop a sense of what you might teach or write about based on the responses you receive. Depending on your goals, it may make sense to approach this as one would approach other major goals as addressed in this book: Draw out milestones to be accomplished, and seek out the feedback of others. This is also a time to renew your commitment to speaking in public and writing. That can take some practice and coaching. Warren Buffett was an introvert who had to overcome a fear of public speaking. "You have to be able to communicate in life and probably schools underemphasize that," he told an interviewer. "If you can't talk to people or write, you're giving up your potential."[2]

Making an assessment of your strengths and purpose is an important step to developing your brand as an expert. I have a few more steps I urge you to consider in making this transition:

- **Is there a business case or a broader aim?** Roughly, are you looking to find new business opportunities, expand your professional brand, cultivate philanthropic activities, improve your industry, or answer community needs?
- **Research your target audience.** Marketing your speaking program, charity, or book through your personal network won't be enough; you'll need to engage communities who have an

existing passion or professional interest in your subject. The key here is to research your market. If you're interested in speaking on personal finance strategies, research the field and read the books on the shelf; if you're a potential leader in a medical specialty, find everything that's been written in peer-reviewed journals. Once you have identified your market ask yourself this: how can I reach these people? My approach was to become a leader in my industry's professional associations. I began by volunteering at the FPA-LA (the Financial Planning Association of Los Angeles), then moved up to the board, and eventually became president. I went on to become president of the West Regional Board of NAPFA (the National Association of Personal Financial Advisors), the fee-only industry association, and serve on the national board. It is interesting to note that I did not start volunteering with the goal of serving as president of these boards. However, I found the camaraderie, experience, and personal growth to be very rewarding.

- **Create a marketing and outreach plan.** Even if it is a grassroots effort, draft and implement (parts of) your thought-leadership plan a year or six months ahead. Do you want to have a greater presence locally? So you need to research local civic, educational, and cultural organizations and network with friends and associates to see where your involvement would be helpful. Do you want to complement your activities with social media such as Facebook or Twitter? If you want to be a Twitter powerhouse, you should know that building a few thousand Twitter followers will probably take at least a year. Are there annual conferences you might speak at? Give speeches at small local venues to get feedback and practice your delivery. Are you thinking about a book? Write a summary of the book and show it to your friends, fans, and followers. Ask for opinions; pose questions; seek their input in your decisions.

- **Consider a marketing partner.** Can you identify an organization, business, or colleague who would benefit from being associated with your efforts? One business author I know realized that to sell his book he needed access to more business seminar opportunities. He reached out to a well-established local finance consultant he knew and offered him a coauthorship. The

new coauthor contributed useful new content without changing the book dramatically and gained a publication credit. In the
end, the two authors developed a joint seminar program aimed
at local businesses.

- **Network in the right place with the right people.** As you
  seek to make larger contributions to your industry and extend
  the influence of your ideas, you'll likely be more involved in
  your local, regional, and national associations and organizations.
  Becoming an expert also requires reaching beyond your familiar
  industry circles, however. Read and explore the best networking
  strategies from authors such as Keith Ferrazzi, in his books *Never
  Eat Alone* and *Who's Got Your Back?* Among his many influential
  ideas for building your social and career network, Ferrazzi teaches
  the importance of developing a circle of trusted relationships and
  friends who help hold us accountable to our goals and values.
  These lifelines introduce and connect us to new contacts in different spheres of life, and act as accountability partners to open new
  doors and make sure we follow through on our commitments.

  And in Porter Gale's highly admired book, *Your Network Is
  Your Net Worth*, you'll learn how knowing your own principles
  and interests is the key to truly magnifying your influence and
  network. By reaching out to connect with new people who share
  your goals and interests you can collaborate in powerful ways. If
  you can find other CPAs who also love classical music or share a
  religious affiliation, what have you, explore those affinity circles.
  Among the many ready-to-use tactics in the book, I like Gale's
  theory of Power Pockets—exploring clubs, professional groups,
  meeting places, and work environments that can accelerate and
  fortify your sense of purpose in reaching new audiences. Attend
  university club events, reunions, go to meet ups, join a local panel,
  play a round of golf at the club where you know a lot of interesting people belong, accept the invite the next time someone offers
  you a chance to see the ballet or a ballgame in the corporate box.[3]

Most of these suggestions are useful even if you're not ready to go
hit the speaking circuit or write your first book. As you become liberated from the dead zone work that made poor use of your time, you'll
have the freedom to think, explore, and express what you've learned

as a business person and a professional. Even writing the occasional article for a local newspaper, joining a board, or speaking at local civic associations or schools will cause people to see you differently and send more referrals your way. You'll discover the ways people see your profession that you and your team likely never thought of amidst the deadlines and meetings. By stepping up your visibility, and doing the homework necessary to back up your ambitions, you keep sharpening your sword.

The biggest mistake you could make, however, is to view this chapter as a veiled plan to market your business and build your client base. While that may be one of many positive outcomes, if you are approaching peers and associations with false pretenses, people will see through you fairly quickly. This is about upping your game, with the primary goal of staying on top of the industry and skills you have strived so hard to master. It is also about giving back and living a well-rounded life.

I had decided a couple years ago that I would use my around-the-world sailing trip to write a book, not only because I had the time, but because I would be regularly meeting new people, getting fresh reactions, and hearing ideas about leadership, management, finance, and financial planning. As I expected, those kinds of interactions churned up additional insights about what we all do in small business, insights that gave me the passion and purpose to write this book. In Porter Gale's *Your Network Is Your Net Worth*, she interviews many highly driven entrepreneurs who reveal that they needed to give more to causes where they could make meaningful contributions, to truly have a high net worth. One typical quote is from Brent Freeman, the CEO of Roozt: "Money is important, so you have freedom, less stress, and don't have to worry about where you get your next meal. But my formula for happiness has many variables that include family, doing well, leaving a legacy, and being a role model and a global citizen."[4]

In discussing core ideas of this book with other professionals, such as attorneys, I have been amazed at how trapped many of them feel as a result of the hourly compensation model most are subject to. This model has other problems beyond those addressed in other chapters. Lawyers and other professionals working under the hourly billing system find it difficult to choose to work part-time—say

20 hours a week—whether for a relatively short period to accommodate other professional interests or long term as part of a comprehensive life change. They find themselves in a feast-or-famine arrangement. This also applies to other employees in the firm, and the result is they cannot build up the systems addressed in this book. Therefore they lack the support necessary to work in their peak zones, where they could work for a smaller percentage of the total time required for a client project, but instead churn hours or get bogged down in dead-zone work.

As a liberated CEO, I've never been more amazed than I am at the conclusion of this trip, by what we can do when we work and produce in our peak zone. That's why we never insist that you follow our program step by step and page by page. Rather we aim to inspire you to think about your business challenges differently, to adopt our ideas and make them your own or take them in entirely new directions. Ultimately we believe any CEO who has experienced what he or she believes is liberation will have touched on all nine strategies in their own way.

★★★

Early in this book, we mentioned bowline knots and the effectiveness and power of their flexibility and strength. We've taught with that metaphor in mind because business is about having the core skills and values that allow you to adapt to constantly changing circumstances while staying strong and reliable through a set of personal and professional principles that are never compromised. We truly believe that the liberated CEO never stops creating value for him- or herself, their firm, family, and larger community from the day they start their practice. The liberated CEO can't do it alone—that's why I urge you to share this book with your family members and colleagues.

Remember, we want to hear about your experiences and views on the ideas in *The Liberated CEO*, and have conversations about what is challenging you on the road to liberation. Visit our website, check out the links to more resources, and start the conversation at:

www.liberatedceo.com

NOTES

1. Don Peppers, "How to Get the Most from a Conference," LinkedIn, www .linkedin.com/today/post/article/20130221134051-17102372-how-to -get-the-most-from-a-conference.
2. Drake Baer, "Lessons from Warren Buffett's Office Hours," interview with Caroline Ghosn, *Fast Company* (blog), www.fastcompany.com/3009443/ bottom-line/5-lessons-from-warren-buffetts-office-hours.
3. Porter Gale, *Your Network Is Your Net Worth* (New York: Atria Books, Simon & Schuster, 2013).
4. Ibid.

CHAPTER 10

AFTERWORD: READY FOR THE NEXT PEAK

I am writing this afterword in the South Pacific archipelago chain of Vanuatu. This unique area has live volcanos where you can stand on the rim and watch the volcano throw lava rocks hundreds of feet into the air. Vanuatu has one of the world's most accessible wreck dives in the world, the World War II supply ship SS *Calvin Coolidge*. We have visited multiple villages with no electricity, running water, or proper sanitation, but their biggest concern is how to charge their cell phones. As you walk among grass huts with no running water or electric lighting, you can hear the ring of cell phones. This diversity and juxtaposition is hitting me with a stark reminder that in less than three months we will be return to living full-time in the United States, when I will be trying not to allow myself to be unliberated by my company, Navigoe.

However, I am also very excited to return. My time away, and the liberation it has provided, has helped me to reignite my entrepreneurial fire. I have also thought a great deal about not only our firm but my entire industry and am eager to start working on a new goal. Small, independent registered investment advisor (RIA) firms, such as mine, are the fastest growing segment of the financial services industry. A 2012 Schwab Advisor Services RIA Benchmarking Study that surveyed over 1,000 firms (the largest of its kind of focusing exclusively on RIAs), found the median RIA firm showed an increase of 13.3 percent in assets

The Leonard family on the rim of a volcano in Vanuatu

under management from 2011 to 2012, with revenue growth of over 7 percent. The study projects that by the end of 2014 about one-third of advisor firms will have doubled in size over the five-year period.[1] And the Occupational Outlook Handbook of the U.S. Department of Labor finds that "employment of personal financial advisors is projected to grow 32 percent from 2010 to 2020, much faster than the average for all occupations. As large numbers of baby boomers approach retirement age, they will seek planning advice from personal financial advisors."

RIA FIRMS IN MAJOR GROWTH TREND

This spectacular growth is creating a lack of replacement talent for the industry. Even with national unemployment over 7 percent, most RIA firms struggle with hiring qualified employees to grow and build a liberated firm. A decade or two ago, one of the most common concerns of my fellow business owners was how to prospect for new clients. Today, one of our industry's largest concerns is how to grow our firms to meet the ever-growing demand for our services.

The success of this small part of the financial services industry shines a bright light on an element of our profession that has gone missing—a professional career path. This situation has been compounded by the creation of financial-planning majors of study in some of the country's best universities. There are a number of graduates from these universities looking for a professional career path, but they still find that the options are almost all limited to either administrative positions or starting their own company.

Comprehensive financial service advisors—financial planning and wealth management—need years of experience to become credentialed and competent to work as a professional advisor. This is not really any different from many other professional service careers. Our problem, in the financial services industry, is the lack of a career path across the industry.

As we discussed back in the first step of becoming a liberated CEO, I am going to share my flight plan with you and start pretesting it for failure. Please feel free to reach out to me with your thoughts, comments, criticisms, and offers to help. I am still in the early planning stages. I am using this afterward to share my plan not only with owners of financial services firms, but with other business owners, too, those whose industries have career paths. What aspects of your industry's process to bring young professionals along in the business are effective and can be replicated? If you could change anything, what would it be?

My idea, and it is just the first draft, is to work with other leading firms like my own, to build a two-year residency for college graduates. During this period, the residents would continue course work to prepare to sit for the two-day comprehensive Certified Financial Planner credential (CFP). Also, during this period, the resident would be gaining the necessary work experience for the CFP.[2]

In part, I see this being built in a way like the first years of public accounting, where many college graduates must work at a public accounting firm, to obtain their Certified Public Accountant (CPA). At that point, less than half of them actually stay in public accounting, but the CPA is an important part of the process necessary to move into many other areas of accounting. The CFP is in many ways trying to replicate the CPA in regard to work experience, testing, and continuing education.

As envisioned today, there would be an agreed upon set of skills that all residents would obtain in their first and second years. To help manage the training time and expense of the firms, the second-year students would be responsible for teaching the first-year students many of the activities. By teaching, they would be going full circle in their mastery of the skill set.

There would be no guarantee of a job with the resident firm at the end of the two years. However, the firms could be working together to share their experiences, and the qualifications of their residents.

Truly liberated firms should find adding this type of residency to be minimally disruptive. The benefit to the firms is that they would get a motivated, well-educated work force that really wants to learn the profession. The benefit to the resident is that not only would they gain the very important two years of work experience, but they would also get to experience the many different roles available in the financial services industry. In a way, both parties are getting to test the other without an expectation of a long-term job offering.

If successful, then the sponsoring firms would be graduating at least one individual a year, who is now a CFP and has experienced many parts of the industry. With proper behavioral tests, such as the Kolbe Index, and a consistent evaluation scheme across the participating firms, the quality of the employee pool would increase for the industry.

There are many details that need to be worked out with this plan. Additionally, there are potential pitfalls that need to be addressed. When I shared this plan with my mother, who is a CPA and also has her MBA, she was concerned that CFPs may face a more limited job pool than CPAs. After the two years of public accounting, once someone has obtained their CPA, they encounter a large number of job options from employers in banking, in-house accounting, tax preparation, and government agencies, that are seeking the new minted CPAs. There is not necessarily the same breadth of companies seeking a CFP as there are seeking a CPA. This is a real issue, and one that needs to be addressed. In the beginning, there are enough firms seeking quality employees that there should be enough supply to meet the demand. However, if successful over time, job supply could become an issue.

If that was in fact the case, there are many other places in the business world where an undergraduate finance degree, along with the CFP and a residency experience, could be highly marketable. Human resources departments would greatly benefit from having CFPs fill management-track HR jobs, for example. Also, there is a very large need in our country for financial-planning advice, delivered free of product sales and other conflicts. The residency program could help train a large number of financial planners to help meet this demand in ways not currently being addressed.

I am mulling other interesting ideas around this goal and I am sharing these as well for the reason that I truly want feedback—and putting these down in the book spurs me to think this out in greater detail. One option would be to actually have the residency program accredited in some manner. This could be accomplished through certificate programs like the CFP, or professional associations such as the Financial Planning Association (FPA) or the National Association of Personal Financial Advisors (NAPFA).

Another could be formal job fair days, or weeks, at the universities that offer majors in financial services. In effect, this would bring the firms and potential residents together for interviews and presentations. As mentioned before, a common set of quarterly evaluations, set up around the different skills and interests of the residents, would help the resident, and future employers, to better understand where an individual would be most likely to succeed in the industry. Conferences could have special tracks for the residences, or even special conferences for residence to help with education and networking.

So now that I have shared with you a goal, or dream, of improving the future of the financial services industry; when you see me, be sure to ask how it is coming along, and hold me to my plan. After all, there is nothing like peer pressure and support to keep you moving toward your goals.

NOTES

1. "Registered Investment Advisors Continue to Set the Pace for Industry Growth, According to Results of the 2013 RIA Benchmarking Study From Charles Schwab," press release, Charles Schwab & Co., July 10, 2013. http://pressroom.aboutschwab.com/press-release/schwab-advisor-services-news/registered-investment-advisors-continue-set-pace-indust-0.
2. The CFP® experience requirement is typically three years; however, a goal would be for this program to meet the CFP Board's two-year apprentice requirement.

APPENDIXES:
LIBERATED CEO
EXTRAS

APPENDIX A

NOTES AND OBSERVATIONS FROM OUR THREE-YEAR GLOBAL SAILING TRIP

The following stories have been adapted from our blog, Three Little Birds, *co-authored by Zoe Alexander.*

I wrote this while crossing the South Pacific from the Galapagos Islands to the Marquesas in French Polynesia—a 20-day trip of nonstop sailing.

I. AN ODE TO TELEMEDICINE

Being away from the United States—and specifically, living on a sailboat with my family—has given me a unique perspective about daily life back home. One of our first concerns we had when planning the trip was how we would address any medical issues that arose at sea. For all the hype about pirates and storms, there is real danger in facing a medical issue in a remote location. Even a minor issue can develop into something major without proper diagnosis or timely treatment.

As our departure date grew closer, the medical question remained unsolved. We thought about taking EMT courses or adventure-care courses, but nothing really seemed to meet our specific needs. We were fortunate to find MedAire, which provides medical kits and training, and MedLink, which is the 24/7 telemedicine service provided through MedAire.

The experience has been a revelation.

The United Sates spends more money per person on health care than almost any other country in the world, but it does not even rank in the top 20 in quality of care. I think we can all agree that this is pretty disturbing. There are numerous reasons, some of them consistent with our values as Americans, but most of our high costs are due to overall inefficiency. As an entrepreneur dedicated to running a tight ship (excuse the pun), and not having immediate access to a medical facility, I've developed a particular interest in this dilemma.

On our boat, we have a vast supply of medications (much of it prescription-strength and controlled medications) in a large suitcase-sized bag called the *ship's medicine chest*, which was sourced by MedAire for our needs (see Figure A.1).

Figure A.1   Contents of Our Ship's Medicine Chest, Stored Separately from the Rest of Our First Aid Equipment in a Secure Location

When someone has an ailment (such as that shown in Figure A.2), we call the medical assistant line, MedLink, via our satellite or cell phone, and experience a traditional office visit over the phone. If medication is necessary, they tell us what we need (since MedLink is a part of MedAire, they know which medical kits we have onboard and where respective meds are located within the kits). They also follow up with multiple e-mails until the issue has been resolved.

As a side note, they also provide us with holistic options if available, which allows us to choose to take the medicine or use a home remedy. We really appreciate this approach because it empowers us with information to make more informed decisions.

We have been impressed with the care we've received because it has been consistently better than care we received in the United States. First off, it's fast. We make contact with a medical professional much sooner than going to our family doctor or waiting in urgent care. Second, it's thorough. The follow up via e-mail is where the quality of care really shines. (When was the last time you visited a doctor and they sent you a follow-up e-mail?)

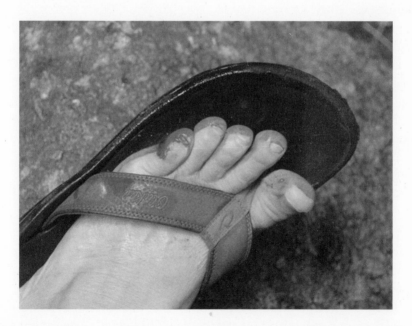

Figure A.2 Hiking in sandals, common when boating. This little mishap was fixed using suture glue with the guidance of MedAire.

And, when you reply, if appropriate, they continue to dialogue until your issue is resolved. Sure, we all appreciate face time, and I am not suggesting that people have a mini-pharmacy at home like we do on our boat. But I know that as a society, we waste a great deal of time and money going to, and dealing with, the many challenges of visiting a doctor's office.

Imagine the many benefits of telemedicine at work. It would help eliminate the time, resources, and energy of driving to the doctor's office—a major benefit for our overall economy. Additionally, your own personalized medical care can be accessed from anywhere in the world. I know that pricks up the ears of those who travel for business or pleasure. Imagine the peace of mind you'd have when faced with a medical challenge away from home knowing help is available over the phone. And, if necessary, a prescription can be e-mailed to a nearby pharmacy. If more people used telemedicine, it would also reduce waiting time in the ER, improving the quality and time frames of care. Take this a step further, and it could decrease the number of doctors at a hospital, allowing more to be on call.

The model for telemedicine is not new. MedLink has been providing excellent care remotely for over 20 years. Not only could this model improve the delivery of health care in the United States, but it could save money too. Fortunately, over the past 12 months we have had no major medical issues, though we have had a vast number of life's smaller ailments one would expect from traveling the Third World via sailboat. And I have come to believe that telemedicine could drastically decrease costs, while improving the quality of medical care provided in the United States. Something to think about. . . .

II. JETLINER TRAVEL KNOW-HOW

I wrote this on my iPad, sitting in the first-class lounge at the international airport in Fiji. Access was gained to the lounge via my American Express Platinum card. While not the most comfortable of lounges, it did have a clean place to sit, with free Wi-Fi and drinks.

There are a large number of websites that help the business traveler make the most of their opportunities. They've helped me a lot but I've also learned a few tricks of my own along the way crisscrossing the world dozens of times in the past five years. Here are a few.

1. **Reward credit cards.** I run as much of the business expenses through my air mileage credit card as possible. There was a time, not too long ago, when American Airlines would allow credit card rewards to count toward your lifetime status. As a result, I am a 2-million-miles member, which gives me lifetime platinum status. I never have a shortage of reward miles to use. The trick is figuring out how to use them.

2. **Reward miles.** At 6′4″, and with a bad back from sports injuries, I really do not like to cram myself into coach seats. As a result, flying business class or higher is critical. I have found the best way to use miles is to actually purchase a coach ticket then use reward miles to upgrade to business class. I have encountered very few times flying in the United States where I have not been able to fly business class using this strategy.

3. **At-the-gate upgrades.** If you travel a good amount, you have probably accumulated a good number of upgrades, which are usually handed out 24 hours before the flight or at the gate. The problem for us business travelers is that we all tend to fly to and from the same places. I frequently find that someone has higher status then I do, so I seldom get to use the upgrades. (That is why I tend to buy coach and use reward miles, as that can be confirmed before you even purchase the ticket.) However, these upgrades are great for vacation travel and for the rest of the family. We will book the family in coach, then put everyone on the upgrade lists. Our kids are now old enough that they can ride in coach while Mandi and I sit in business.

One funny story comes to me, back when the kids were pretty young, and Luke was still traveling on the airplane in a car seat. We were on our way home from Hawaii, a notoriously difficult route to upgrade. When we were preparing to board the plane, it became obvious that only two of our party of five was upgraded. When we told the boys that they would not be sitting with us, one of them exclaimed loudly, "You mean I have to fly in *second* class?"

We waited until the latest moment to board, and while Mandi situated herself in business class, I went to help get the boys arranged in coach. I set up Luke's car seat in the window seat, made sure the other two boys were squared away, and then walked back up to business class. The looks on the passengers' faces were as expected; a mix between horror and utter astonishment that we would leave our three young boys, one still a toddler, alone with them in coach. However, we have traveled enough with our children to know that they are better than most adults when flying. After being deprived of video games for a month before the trip, they are happy to quietly sit and play their Nintendo Game Boys for hours.

Just to finish out the thought of traveling with young kids—while it is a hassle, bring along the child's car seat on the plane. Kids are used to sitting in their car seats for extended periods, so they are more inclined to be locked into their car seat on the plane and not need to squirm and want to get up and walk around. They may even fall asleep, since they know from experience that once locked into that seat, they are there for the duration.

4. **Super-secret booking trick.** If you really want to be able to maximize the likelihood of using your upgrades, you need to befriend an employee of the airline who has access to their employee-reservation system. This system will tell you how full a plane is, the number of people on upgrade lists, the status of those people, and so on. If you are a little flexible in your travel plans, you could be able to fly business, or even first class, on all your flights.

III. PAPA SHERPA'S FIVE GOLDEN RULES OF TRAVELING AROUND THE WORLD WITH KIDS

One of a Sherpa's jobs deals with the logistics of moving all the stuff necessary for an expedition. In our family, that role falls to me, hence the term Papa Sherpa. We have traveled a lot as a family, ever since Griffin was six months old when we took a two-week surf vacation to a remote part of Mexico. Our boys have club memberships on an airline and are already on their second passports. This experience inspired me to create my five Golden Rules of Travel for our family.

Figure A.3 If Your Kids Like the Food, Don't Ask What It Is

1. **Never miss an opportunity to use the bathroom.** I know, sounds simple. Whenever we pick up a rental car with bathrooms nearby and I ask if anyone needs to use the restroom before we leave, I hear "No, we're fine." Then, 10 minutes later when we're on the road, the kids chime in, "I have to use the bathroom!" You can imagine the conversation from there, "We were at a bathroom 10 minutes ago!" "I didn't need to go then . . ." "Then you mustn't need to go that bad, you can wait." "No, I have to go really bad!" So, if we pass a bathroom, everyone goes, whether they have to or not.

2. **If you like it, don't ask what it is.** This rule, as with the rest, relates to food (see Figure A.3). If you have done any international travel with small children, you will embrace this one quickly. Keeping young kids fed while traveling can be very difficult. And nothing is more defeating than having the kids try something new, like it, but then discover what it is, and suddenly state that they can no longer eat it. There is a reason we don't tour a sausage factory, or go to the slaughterhouse when visiting a farm. If your child eats a food they like, encourage them to just be happy and eat it. And the next time your child asks you what they are eating, reply, "Chicken."

3. **Don't fight the menu.** If there is a Chef's Special, it is usually pretty good. Don't try and redesign it; it's been prepared a certain way for a reason. Be open-minded and experiment. The locals know what is good and fresh. If you try to customize your order, it should be no surprise then—especially when language is an issue—that it never comes out right. Just point to the Chef's Special and you'll be fine.

4. **Lime fixes many ills.** I learned this one traveling around Central and South America. Lime kills germs, which is why it was rubbed around the lip of beer. It also has a pretty distinctive flavor, which can mask many bad tastes. When the Chef's Special (prepared by the mother of a local family who has invited you to dinner) is different than what you are used to, lime can really help. Order lime with your beer, and keep it around for dinner.

5. **Bacon makes everything taste better.** I don't think this needs any explanation. If it is on the menu, and it has bacon in the description, it trumps the Chef's Special. Eat it.

IV. WIRELESS COMMUNICATIONS AT SEA

During 2012 and into 2013, we sailed from the east coast of the United States through the Caribbean, across Panama, and into the South Pacific, as I continued to run my company, Navigoe, remotely from the boat. The need to remain in constant e-mail and phone contact with Navigoe has given me a great deal of experience in remote broadband communications.

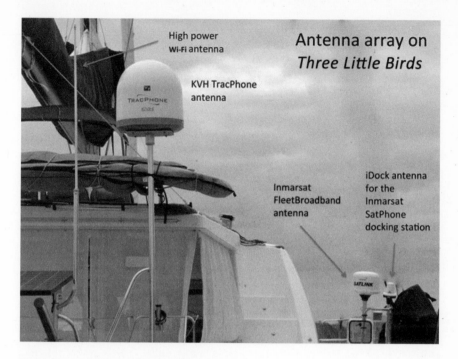

Figure A.4 The Ship's Communications Array

There are numerous factors to evaluate when considering a global communications system for a boat; the most important is a realistic analysis of your individual requirements. The next biggest factors to consider are speed of connectivity and the amount of data to be consumed. And embedded within these two factors are the timeliness of the speed and your data requirements. In other words, do you need to send a great deal of data on demand, or can you get by with very little data and wait until you can find a shore-based solution to send larger files? The next factors to consider are your sailing destinations and budget.

Cell Phones

Almost every little town you'll sail by, or anchor near, has cell coverage. You can always use your home country phone in a pinch, or get an international-roaming package for better pricing. Another affordable and efficient option is having a world cell phone that allows you to change SIM cards and use the cell services of the local provider.

Having a world cell phone that can set up its own Wi-Fi hot spot is also very useful for leveraging local 3G service on the boat. This is really handy if you stay in a location for any length of time—and critical if you want to communicate with locals who may be working on your boat.

Many of the islands in the West Indies have full 3G coverage, and data plans are fairly priced. You may find that your home cell phone roaming prices for calls and SMS are not that bad, but don't expect locals to call your U.S. cell phone number. A good multifunction smart phone can allow for decent, high-speed, broadband access. In the South Pacific, cell coverage is still available near towns, but no real broadband service is available with the phones.

Handheld Satellite Phone

We have the Inmarsat's IsatPhone Pro. Since this phone needs a clear view of the sky to get reception, we added an iBeam docking station, which has an external antenna, allowing for coverage (see Figure A.4). Try to think of these phones as providing calling and SMS services only. Even though they can be connected to a computer for data transfer, they get very expensive. Calling costs depend on the plan you purchase, with prices ranging from $0.30 to $1 a minute. As with your U.S.-based cell phone, incoming text messages are free, which can be a great way to leverage your communications with people back home.

Inmarsat's FleetBroadband

This service is a metered-usage plan with broadband, so sending a great deal of data can get very expensive quickly. This service requires you to sign up for a plan with monthly usage allotments, very similar to a cell-phone plan. The equipment needed, both the antenna and the modem, is very small, and can be installed easily on most boats. Ours is a 12-volt DC unit, which is also better with power consumption, and simple to install compared with the 110-volt systems. Coverage by Inmarsat is truly worldwide.

KVH's Mini-VSAT Trackphone

This service has both metered plans and all-you-can-eat, unlimited phone and data plans, so you pay for the speed of the broadband connection. The equipment for this service is relatively large, and both the antenna and the modem are very expensive. It is also a 110-volt system, so installation and electrical requirements are more complicated. The coverage is *not* worldwide.

Communications for *Three Little Birds*

Our first step was setting up all the land-based options on our boat. We have an antenna that can reach out and grab shore-based Wi-Fi. In the Caribbean, this was very helpful, as the connection speed was much faster than our satellite connection. We also have a worldwide phone and can purchase a SIM card if we need to be able to talk with locals, or use a cellular data plan for e-mail. We also have the handheld IsatPhone as a backup. But since it requires an unobstructed view of the sky, it was not used much until we added the iDock.

To complement this, we added the KVH mini-VSAT system with an unlimited usage plan. I was not sure how much connectivity I would need (or want), so my decision was really based on a service that would allow for unlimited access. This was a major installation due to the size of the antenna and wiring requirements. We worked with MPI Marine Professionals in Fort Lauderdale, Florida, for the installation. They did a great job. Going in, I knew we wouldn't have coverage once we left Panama and sailed into the South Pacific, but at the time, the desire for unlimited data usage was the deciding factor.

Once we went through the Panama Canal, the need to find another solution to our KVH mini-VSAT system became urgent. So, at the last minute we decided to add the Inmarsat FleetBroadband. Due to the small antenna and the modem, we were able to do the installation at anchor in Panama City with no special fabrication necessary for the antenna. We worked with a local firm for the installation of the hardware in Panama, which was arranged and managed by the MVS Group back in the United States. Our experience with MVS has been great. They are extremely responsive via e-mail and helpful in every manner possible.

We also installed the iDock for the IsatPhone for 24/7 service. This allows the office to send me SMS messages (for free) anytime, indicating when we should turn on the FleetBroadband system and access our e-mail.

KVH versus Inmarsat Broadband

When we started with the KVH mini-VSAT, it was great to have unlimited data access, especially with five people on the boat. However, the plan was very expensive, as was the installation and the equipment.

- *Pricey.* Before we departed, we did not realize how extensive the cellular services are in the Caribbean and the amount of Wi-Fi hotspots set up specifically for boaters in the major anchorages. In hindsight, we would have been better off to take a less expensive satellite option—FleetBroadband—and use the money saved on local SIM cards, data plans, and Wi-Fi options.
- *Slow.* We were very, very disappointed with the speed of our plan. While we paid for a mid-speed plan, we actually never received the speeds we paid for and were very disappointed by the service—or lack thereof—when we tried to get this resolved with technical support.
- *Sticky plans.* Although we signed up for a one-year plan, we could not downgrade to less expensive, slower connectivity in an attempt to pay for the speeds we were actually getting. We were paying for broadband speeds one would expect with a 3G phone, but were getting close to old-school dial up. As a result, we used shore-based Wi-Fi whenever possible, which was most places.
- To add insult to injury, the plan would not let us access YouTube. Their argument was that we are not allowed to stream media—which wasn't an issue since the connection was so slow anyway. We tried to explain that we needed access to the site to manage our own YouTube account, not to stream video. But they would not allow access, even though there are many other sites that stream video that we could access. This arbitrary, inflexible policy illustrates the overall lack of customer support at KVH.

Inmarsat FleetBroadband

Phone coverage is excellent, as with the KVH mini-VSAT system. Our Internet access speed is good, actually better than what we received with the KVH mini-VSAT.

- *Efficient.* We were also very impressed with how it used about one-third the electricity and was able to connect with the satellite in about half the time, as compared with the mini-VSAT system solution. In a perfect world, the FleetBroadband would have an all-you-can-eat option too.
- *Affordable.* For less than one-third of what we paid monthly for the mini-VSAT system, we are able to get the necessary e-mail communications and daily weather files downloaded. While in the Galapagos Islands, we ate out almost every lunch and dinner so we could enjoy the free Wi-Fi access in restaurants. This was still less expensive than our old mini-VSAT plan with the added benefit of a nice meal.

With the Inmarsat plan, I am able to maintain the connectivity necessary to run my business remotely. What we have given up is the unlimited access we enjoyed before.

In Hindsight

Doing it all over again, I would skip the KVH mini-VSAT system and go directly with the Inmarsat FleetBroadband. The difference in cost for hardware and installation alone would have saved us tens of thousands of dollars, which could have been applied to purchasing more data, either via satellite or cellular. An unlimited satellite option would be nice as we sit in a totally deserted atoll in the Tuamatu archipelago for a week (where there are no cell or Wi-Fi options), but the KVH mini-VSAT system does not cover this area anyway.

Along the way, I also found the MVS Group, who were great in helping me figure out how to best address my needs as we sailed into the Pacific. I am sure that if I had contacted them before the trip began, I would not have made the mistake of starting with the mini-VSAT.

There are systems out there I haven't tried. There is the Sailmail option with shortwave radio—we don't have one so I can't weigh in on that. Also, we know of some people who are using the BGAIN system with portable terminals (also with the Inmarsat service) with success. BGAIN is not designed for access when the boat is moving, as the antenna is fixed; however, at anchor or on shore it can provide an affordable broadband solution when Wi-Fi is not available.

For those whose access can wait until they are near land (we are at anchor around 90 percent of the time), cellular communications with Wi-Fi options could be your sole system—especially in the West Indies. Support this with either an Inmarsat handheld phone in an iDock or a FleetBroadband system, and you should be ready to go anyplace. I am just hoping I can find someone to trade the V7 TracPhone for a marine satellite TV antenna so I can watch some Lakers games!

V. THE BALANCING ACT

I wrote this earlier in the trip, and my views haven't changed in that time. The benefits of combining business and parenting can be enjoyed in many different scenarios—and are all part of living as a liberated CEO.

It's easier than I thought to mix work and family during these first months of the trip. As our lives are much simpler—no after-school commitments, TV, or play dates—we have more time to spend together. After dinner, we take walks along the beach.

Technology has really liberated me in how I approach a work/life balance. My office on the boat resembles a little nook at the Mac store. I am connected to the California office via my iMac, iPad, and iPhone. Being connected this way enables me to handle the boat and the kids while being available to the office. This multitasking energizes me because it keeps my contact with the business lean and focused, and I am able to participate in most of the boys' daily activities. Our days are structured around their school, which starts promptly at 8:00 A.M. Jake and Griffin have math class first, so I sit between them, read the *Wall Street Journal* on my iPad, have coffee, and help them when needed.

A big part of our day is spent at the family table, either with school or meals, and it is where the Leonard family multitasks best. We eat most meals together, so we use that time to review school assignments. Many of the boys' assignments provide discussion sections, so Mandi and I lead the discussion topics, and the boys bounce ideas off of us, as well as each other. This process has helped build critical thinking skills in the boys—a valuable ability to encourage at any age. The round-table nature of these discussions also really helps ensure that they grasp the material.

We have always been an active family, and discovered that morning exercise helps the boys sit through school. That job has fallen to me. Also, during the school day, we try to take a recess to expend some more energy. Again, my job. And it's a win-win because I get to exercise with the boys. Yeah, I could drink coffee and greet the day in front of a screen, but this routine brings harmony to the day. Some of the activities we enjoy are walking around the local towns, kayaking, stand-up paddleboard, Pilates on the boat, swimming, snorkeling, and water polo.

One of the best parts of our trip—by design—is that there are so few life distractions that we just spend time together. I love walking down the beach at night, holding hands with my boys. Or when we sail at night and one of the boys can't sleep, we watch the stars and contemplate life on other planets. And, after we put the boys to sleep, Mandi and I have time to be together to talk. Sounds simple, but we rarely did that on land—we were either too busy or too tired. Striking a work/family balance involves navigating each day by what is truly important, and being able to wear many hats. You'd be surprised how efficient balance can be if you take time to think it through. Trust me, it's worth it.

To learn more:
- *Three Little Birds* blog: http://threelittlebirds.org/
- *Three Little Birds* Facebook page: https://www.facebook.com/sailingontlb
- Q&A with Scott Leonard, *Southern Boating* magazine: http://southernboating.com/blog/2011/08/11/e-newsletter-qa-scott-leonard-the-mobile-ceo/

APPENDIX B

FURTHER READING AND RELATED RESOURCES

You can visit the Navigoe website and blog at: www.navigoe.com.

To learn more from the expert consultants discussed in the book:

- The Kolbe Corporation, www.kolbe.com. Kathy Kolbe, founder, David Kolbe, CEO, and Amy Bruske, president. P: 602-840-9770 E: info@kolbe.com.
- Gallup Strategic Consulting, www.gallup.com/strategiccons ulting/en-us/main.aspx?ref=b.
- Clifton StrengthsFinder, www.gallup.com/strategicconsulting/ 157208/achieving-greater-performance-strengths.aspx.
- Career Anchors Self-Assessment, www.careeranchorsonline .com/SCA/about.do?open=prod.
- My Virtual COO, www.myvirtualcoo.com/. Jennifer Goldman, president. Contact: info@myvirtualcoo.com.
- Texas de Brazil, www.texasdebrazil.com/. "10 Tips for Great Grilling from Texas de Brazil Culinary Director, Evandro Caregnato," www.texasdebrazil.com/menu/meats.

- Books and DVDs by Tony Buzan, www.tonybuzan.com/books/.
- Mark C. Tibergien, CEO and managing director, Pershing Advisory Solutions, LLC, www.pershing.com/about_us/mark_tibergien.html.
- Rebecca Pomering, CEO and principal, Moss Adams Wealth Advisors, www.mossadamswealthadvisors.com/About-Us/Our-Team/Rebecca-Pomering.
- Dan Seivert, CEO and Managing Partner, Echelon Partners, investment bankers, wealth consultants, and valuation experts, Dan Seivert, CEO and Managing Partner, www.echelon-partners.com/.

To explore the resources of professional services associations:

- Financial Planning Association, www.fpanet.org/; FPA events and conferences site for professionals: www.fpanet.org/professionals/EventsConferences/Conferences/; FPA regional chapters, www.fpanet.org/professionals/Connect/Chapters/; The FPA's great practice management blog, http://practicemanagementblog.fpanet.org/.
- The National Association of Personal Financial Advisors, www.napfa.org/; NAPFA events, www.napfa.org/conferences/NAPFAEvents.asp.
- Certification resources: CFP Board is a nonprofit organization acting in the public interest by fostering professional standards in personal financial planning through its setting and enforcement of the education, examination, experience, ethics, and other requirements for CFP certification. www.cfp.net/home.
- American Bar Association, www.americanbar.org/aba.html.
- American Medical Association, www.ama-assn.org/ama.
- American Accounting Association, http://aaahq.org/.
- National Society of Accountants, www.nsacct.org/.
- Association of Management Consulting Firms, www.amcf.org/.

Customer relationship management (CRM) software:

- *PC Magazine*'s CRM reviews and resources, www.pcmag.com/products/1627.
- Salesforce.com, www.salesforce.com/.
- Microsoft Dynamics, www.microsoft.com/en-us/dynamics/crm.aspx?WT.srch=1&WT.mc_ID=DYNAMICS_US_SEM_GA.
- Zoho CRM, www.zoho.com/crm/.

Great business books and information resources for the entrepreneur:

- Stephen Covey, *The 7 Habits of Highly Effective People*, Free Press/ Simon & Schuster, www.stephencovey.com/7habits/7habits.php.
- Keith Ferrazzi, *Who's Got Your Back?* Crown/Random House, http://keithferrazzi.com/products/whos-got-your-back.
- Porter Gale, *Your Network Is Your Net Worth*, Atria/Simon & Schuster, www.portergale.com/your-network-is-your-net-worth-book/.
- Michael Gerber, *The E-Myth Revisited* and other E-Myth books, HarperBusiness, www.michaelegerbercompanies.com/ resources/products/.
- Joseph Michelli, *The New Gold Standard: 5 Leadership Principles for Creating a Legendary Customer Experience Courtesy of the Ritz-Carlton Hotel Company*, McGraw-Hill, www.josephmichelli .com/index.php?pg=4&PHPSESSID=031f63c07394ee9673b23 263f9c23e93.
- Alice Schroeder, *The Snowball: Warren Buffett and the Business of Life*, Bantam, www.amazon.com/The-Snowball-Warren-Buf fett-Business/dp/0553384619.

I highly recommend the research, papers, and publications of the Kauffman Foundation:

- Data and surveys: www.kauffman.org/researchandpolicy/entre preneurship-data.aspx.
- Entrepreneurship tools, strategies, applied knowledge: www .kauffman.org/Section.aspx?id=Entrepreneurship.
- Education: www.kauffman.org/Section.aspx?id=Education.

Areas where Navigoe uses outsourced consultants and experts:

Marketing
- Web design
- Search-engine optimization (SEO)
- E-mail marketing
- Social-media consultant
- Blog

Compliance
- Compliance consultant
- E-mail monitoring and retention
- CRM process to remind our compliance officer to do necessary reviews

Legal
- Compliance
- Corporate agreements
- Client agreements

Accounting
- Bookkeeping
- CFO level consulting and strategy
- Accounting firm for tax preparation and strategy

ABOUT THE AUTHOR

Scott Leonard, CFP®, is the owner of Navigoe, Inc., a registered investment advisor (RIA) with offices in Nevada and California. He was the sole founder and owner of Leonard Wealth Management Inc., established in 1996, as an all-inclusive wealth management firm, which became Navigoe in 2013. Scott was listed as one of the five most influential registered investment advisors for 2013.

Scott maintained his executive role at his firm during his planned three-year trip sailing from Florida to Australia, making quarterly flights to the United States for client meetings. Scott has been an instructor at UCLA Extension, teaching courses in the financial planning certificate program. He has also been an instructor and dean of the School of Investments for NAPFA University. He is a national speaker on investment, wealth management, and practice management issues. Scott is a published author, specializing in advanced investment theory, and has been the featured financial planner for the *Los Angeles Times* weekly "Money Make-Over" column. His analysis and opinions on advanced wealth management issues are featured in national publications, including the *Wall Street Journal, USA Today, Money Magazine,* and *Kiplinger's Personal Finance.*

Scott graduated from the University of California, Los Angeles (UCLA) in 1990 with a bachelor of science degree in economics. His CFP® credential was earned in 1994.

INDEX